A MUSICAL FEAST

Recipes from over 100 of the world's most famous musical artists

compiled by Wendy Diamond

Global Liaisons, Incorporated/Publishers New York

Published in 1995 by Global Liaisons Incorporated.
P.O. Box 6049, New York, New York 10150

A Musical Feast : Recipes from over 100 of the world's most famous musical artists compiled by Wendy Diamond. — 1st edition.

This book was published as a fund raiser to combat homelessness. Seventy percent of Global Liaisons, Incorporated's profit will be donated to the following organizations: Coalition for the Homeless, New York. Empty the Shelters, National Coalition for the Homeless, San Francisco Coalition on Homelessness.

Most of the recipes contained in this book have been tested and edited from their original form. Some recipes have been maintained in their original form to reflect the personality of the artist who contributed that particular recipe. Global Liaisons, Incorporated, the Homeless organizations and sponsors take no responsibility for any liability arising out of any injury of any kind which may be sustained from participation in or connection with the making or utilization of the recipes included in this publication.

Publisher & Art Director, Wendy Diamond
Senior designer, Carl A. Sharif
Contributing Designers; Vanos, Lou Lumarno
Recipe editor, Lori Lynn Narlock
Contributing editors, Randy Blunk, Libby Parella, Catharine Williams
Non-profit liaison, Hilary Diamond
Artist Index contributed by Rolling Stone Press; Holly George Warren, editor.
Shawn Dahl, associate editor. Greg Emmanuel, editorial assistant.
Cover illustration, Will Cypser and Jim Fletcher

Library of Congress Catalog Card Number: 95-78322

ISBN 0-9647316-0-6

Table
of Contents

Menu

PHOTO AND ILLUSTRATION CREDITS

Table of Contents......................*photo Barry Hart*
Kitchen of Bernie Cyrus, Louisiana Music Commissioner

Aerosmith, Steven Tyler.........*photo Michael Halsband*
Joe Perry ....*photo Gene Kirkland*
Allman Brothers, Warren Haynes ......*photo Wendy Diamond*
Allman Brothers..........................*photo Kirk West*
Anderson, Laurie......................*photo Kevin Mazur*
Beach Boys ....*illustration Joe Riviera*
Bennett, Tony ....*photo Kevin Mazur*
Bon Jovi.................................*border Billy Karesh*
David Bryan.....................*photo April Bryan, his wife*
Richie Sambora..........................*photo Nick Moyle*
Tico Torres............................*photo Philipe Lerale*
Byrne, David......................*illustration Robert Risko,*
background Billy Karesh
Cash, Johnny, June Carter .... *photo Ebet Roberts*
The Chieftains ....*photo Caroline Greyshock*
Cyrus, Billy Ray ....*photo Beth Gwinn*
D. Heavy...............................*photo his mother*
Diamond, Wendy ....*photo Mychal Watts*
Diddley, Bo..............................*photo Chris Tuthill*
Dr. John..............................*photo Stanley Chaisson*
Etheridge, Melissa ....*photo Neal Preston*
Gabriel, Peter ....*photo Ed Quinn*
Gill, Vince.................................*photo Beth Gwinn*
Hootie and the Blowfish..............*photo Mark Zenow*
King, B.B.................................*photo Kevin Mazur*
Knight, Gladys............................*photo David Roth*
Kool and the Gang....................*photo Carol Marino*
LaBelle, Patti.........................*photo Amelia Panico*
Loeb, Lisa ....*photo Chris Bierlan and Bennett Miller,*
makeup Pam Taylor
Loveless, Patty..........................*photo Neal Preston*
Lovett, Lyle..............................*photo David Rose*
Mack, Craig...........................*photo Carol Marino*
Madonna ....*illustration Al Hughes*
McCartney, Paul and Linda...........*photo Kevin Mazur*
McLachlan, Sarah...........................*photo Al Robb*
Meat Loaf...................*illustration Michael Cebollero*
Minnelli, Liza...................*illustration Michael Kaluta*
Moby...................................*photo Jason Block*

Nelson, Willie ....*illustration Al Hughes*
The Neville Brothers...............*photo Johnathon Postal*
Parton, Dolly..........................*illustration Al Hughes*
Peter, Paul and Mary ....*photo Donald Pong*
Reed, Lou ....*photo Kevin Mazur,*
background photo Coleen Devine
Reeves, Dianne.....................*photo Victor Malafrante*
Restless Heart ....*photo Alan Mayor*
Rogers, Roy ....*photo Beth Gwinn*
RuPaul ....*photo David Rose*
Spin Doctors ....*photo Paul La Rosa*
Sponge ....*photo Michael Halsband*
Sonic Youth.........................*photo Mike Hashimoto*
Soul Asylum...........................*photo Matt Mahurin*
Stuart, Marty ....*photo Beth Gwinn*
The Marleys (Rita and Ziggy) ......*photo Sharon Marley*
The Rolling Stones............*oil on canvas Ronnie Wood*
They Might Be Giants ....*photo Aldo Mauro*
Tillis, Pam................................*photo Beth Gwinn*
Tritt, Travis.............................*photo Beth Gwinn*
Weezer ....*photo Aldo Mauro*
Wild Colonials ....*photo Lee Cantelon*
Wynette, Tammy ....*photo Beth Gwinn*

Thanks to the following companies for the usage of their stock photos: Corel, Digital Stock and Photodisc. APS Technologies, Digital Storage and Syquest for their donations of computer hardware and software.

AUTHOR'S NOTE

Congratulations! You've contributed towards solving the problem of homelessness by purchasing *A MUSICAL FEAST*.

The idea for creating this book came to me over Thanksgiving weekend, 1993. I volunteered at the Bowery mission in New York City, where I served meals to the homeless. I was so struck by what I had seen that I wanted to make a lasting contribution. That day I realized that homelessness is not just a seasonal problem, but a problem 365 days a year. Thousands of people in the United States are homeless, without a bed to sleep in, food to eat, or even a warm jacket to wear.

That was the inspiration for this book. I did not know any musical artists or even know how to cook when I started. I knew that if I could reach the world's leading musical artists, they would donate their own favorite recipes, illustrations and photos to this cookbook that benefits organizations dedicated to helping the homeless.

The first to respond were Paul and Linda McCartney with their recipe for Chili non carne (vegetarian chili). Over the next year, I gained the support of more than one hundred artists. The greatest feeling was when the recipes started coming in, recipes like Madonna's family recipe for Cherry Torte, Melissa Etheridge's Healthy Rice and Bean Soup and Tony Bennett's mother's secrets to cooking.

Proceeds benefit four organizations dedicated to helping the homeless: Empty The Shelters, National Coalition for the Homeless, Coalition for the Homeless, New York, and Coalition on Homelessness San Francisco.

The artists who have contributed creative and personal recipes, the beautifully illustrated pages, and most importantly, the benefit to the homeless, make *A MUSICAL FEAST* the hippest cookbook ever published!

Thanks to everyone who participated, and to you, the reader, for your support!

Eat Well, Be Happy!

ACE OF BASE

This is the favorite recipe of Ulf "Buddha" Eckberg.

Chicken in a Clay Pot, Served with Roasted Potatoes and Gravy

1	2 1/2-pound chicken
	Juice of 1 lemon
1	teaspoon paprika
1	teaspoon dried basil
	Salt and pepper, to taste

Pour lemon juice over chicken, season with paprika, basil and salt and pepper. Place chicken in clay pot; cover with lid. Place pot in cold oven. Turn oven to 400°F. Bake for 1 hour.

Roasted Potatoes

6	potatoes, peeled and sliced 1/2-inch thick
2	tablespoons lemon juice
4	tablespoons melted butter
	Salt and pepper, to taste

Place potato slices in baking dish and cover with lemon juice. Brush melted butter over potatoes and season with salt and pepper. Place in oven with chicken and bake 50 minutes. Baste with additional melted butter, once or twice while cooking.

Gravy

4	tablespoons butter
4	tablespoons all-purpose flour
	Liquid from chicken pot, add water to yield 2 cups
1/2	cube vegetable stock
1/2	cube chicken stock
1/2	cube beef stock
3	tablespoons brandy
	White and black pepper, to taste
	Paprika, to taste.
1/2	cup heavy cream

Melt butter in small saucepan. Add flour to butter, stirring to make a smooth paste. Add liquid, stock cubes, and brandy. Stir until well blended. Season with peppers and paprika. Bring to boil, remove from heat and let cool. Add cream; heat and serve over chicken and potatoes.

6 Servings

The Allman Brothers Band

Candied Yams á la Warren Haynes With a lot of help from Sandra Wright

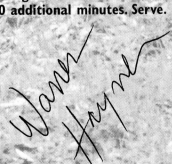

4	large sweet potatoes, sliced
1/2	cup brown sugar
1/2	cup Karo® syrup
1/2	cup (1 stick) butter, melted

Preheat oven to 250°F.

Place potato slices in baking dish. Cover with brown sugar. Bake 45 minutes. Remove from oven and cover with Karo syrup and butter. Bake 30 additional minutes. Serve.

8 Servings

Warren Haynes

Joe Perry's
Vegetable Vindaloo

On tour around the world, wherever that may be, I am a true fan of Spicy foods.

1	tablespoon olive oil
2	medium onions, diced
2	medium potatoes, peeled and diced
1	tablespoon fresh ginger, minced
3	tablespoons curry powder or paste
	(this recipe was named for the brand I use—Vindalo
2	large carrots, sliced
2	small zucchini, sliced Handful of cauliflower florets
1	8-ounce can tomato paste
1	cup water
1	cup frozen peas
1/2	teaspoon wine vinegar
	Ground chili pepper, to taste

Heat oil in a large skillet. Add onions, potatoes, and ginger; cook until onions become translucent. Season with curry powder/paste, adding more olive oil, if mixture becomes dry, continue to cook over medium heat about 5 minutes.

Add carrots, zucchini, cauliflower, tomato paste and water; bring to boil.
Cover and simmer 10 minutes, until vegetables are tender. Stir in peas, vinegar and chili pepper. Cook until peas are heated.
It's ready to serve!

Serving Suggestions:

Vegetable Vindaloo can be served with basmati rice, eaten on its own or used as a side dish with any number of delicious Indian main courses, such as tandoori chicken. Great accompaniments to Vegetable Vindaloo are lime pickle and sweet mango chutney.
And if you don't eat everything you've made in one sitting, remember...
it's even better cold the next day!

4 Servings

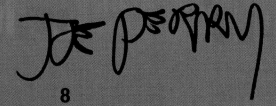

Steven Tyler Bombay noodles with Peanut Sauce

I eat a banana everyday for good luck and because I'm healthy!

1	banana
1	pound noodles, cooked al dente'
1/3	cup hot water
1/3	cup smooth peanut butter
2	teaspoons soy sauce
2	teaspoons white vinegar
2	scallions, finely chopped,
1	tablespoon reserved
2	garlic cloves, minced
1	tablespoon sugar
1/4	teaspoon hot red pepper flakes (I usually add a lot more!)

Eat the banana.

Combine hot water and peanut butter, until completely blended. Add soy sauce, vinegar, scallions, garlic, sugar and hot pepper.

Add sauce to hot pasta in a large serving bowl. Toss to coat pasta completely. Garnish with reserved scallions. Chow Down!

4 Servings

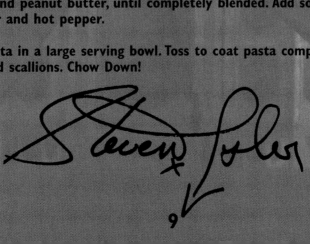

Arrested Development

Speech's favorite recipes:
Fried Catfish, Red Beans and Rice, and Fresh Cabbage
As prepared by Mrs. B. (Bernard Ellington),
Speech's favorite cook in Atlanta.

Fried Catfish

2	pounds catfish fillet
3	tablespoons Tabasco® pepper sauce
1/4	cup fish-fry mix
	(Mrs. B. uses Louisiana Fish Fry; it's all natural and there's no salt added)
1	teaspoon salt
	teaspoon pepper

Heat vegetable oil (2 to 3 inches deep) in large skillet. Wash fish thoroughly in cold water. Brush each fillet with Tabasco® sauce, then coat with fish-fry mix, season with salt and pepper. Place coated fillets in hot oil and cook until golden brown. Remove from pan and place on paper towels to absorb excess oil. Serve. ENJOY.

2 Servings

Red Beans and Rice

1	16-ounce package dried kidney beans
1	tablespoon vegetable oil
1	medium onion, chopped
1	medium green bell pepper, diced
2	garlic cloves, minced
2	cups uncooked rice
1	teaspoon salt

Rinse and sort beans. Bring 6 cups of cold water to boil in large pot. Add beans, bring to boil, cook 2 minutes. Remove from heat, cover and soak 1 hour. Drain and rinse. Fill heavy large Dutch oven with 6 cups hot water. Bring to boil. Add beans, let simmer gently 1 1/2 to 2 hours (do not boil on high heat or beans will burst). Heat oil in large skillet. Add onion, bell pepper and garlic, cook until tender, about 4 minutes. Drain beans, reserving liquid. Add water to reserved liquid to yield 4 cups. Place liquid in heavy large Dutch oven; add beans, onion mixture, rice and salt. Bring to boil, reduce heat, cover and simmer 15 minutes (do not lift cover or stir). Remove from heat. Fluff with fork; cover and let sit 5 to 10 minutes. Serve.

8 to 12 Servings

Fresh Cabbage

2	tablespoons vegetable oil
2	scallions with tops, chopped
1/2	medium bell pepper, diced
2	garlic cloves, chopped
1	medium head green cabbage, shredded
1	teaspoon salt
1/8	teaspoon pepper (black or red)

Heat oil in heavy large Dutch oven. Add onion, bell pepper and garlic. Sauté 3 minutes. Add 1 cup water, cabbage, salt and pepper. Cover and bring to boil; reduce heat. Simmer 10 minutes. Strain liquid from cabbage mixture and discard.

4 to 6 Servings

AKA Speech

BABY FACE

Kenny & Tracey Edmonds

Every baby's Spicy Chicken

4	tomatoes, diced
1/4	cup white vinegar
2	tablespoons Tabasco® pepper sauce
	Salt and pepper, to taste
20	chicken wings, washed and patted dry

Preheat oven to 350° F.

Mix together tomatoes, vinegar, Tabasco, salt, and pepper in large bowl. Bend small part of wing to overlap large part, to prevent opening while baking. Add chicken to tomato mixture, cover thoroughly. Marinate chicken 20 minutes. Place chicken on a large baking sheet; bake 45 minutes, uncovered.

6 Servings

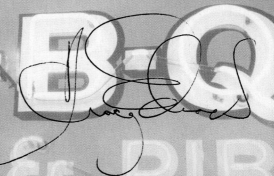

Anita Baker

Corn Chowder

3	tablespoons unsalted butter
1	large onion, chopped
4	cups chicken stock
1	cup yellow cornmeal
1/2	cup fresh lemon juice
4	cups fresh sweet corn
	Salt and freshly ground pepper, to taste
1/2	cup chopped chives

Melt butter in heavy large saucepan. Add onion and sauté until soft, about 10 minutes. Add stock and simmer over low heat, about 30 minutes. Gradually whisk in cornmeal until mixture becomes thick, about 5 minutes.

Using blender or food processor, puree the cornmeal mixture. Strain through fine sieve. Return to saucepan, add lemon juice and corn. Cook over medium heat until corn is tender, about 5 minutes. Season with salt and pepper. Divide into bowls and garnish with chives.

3 Servings

BASIA

Polish Bigos

I	pound sauerkraut, prepared, chopped
I	pound cabbage, chopped
I	tablespoon vegetable oil
I	large onion, sliced
1/2	pound pork, beef, chicken, or Polish kielbasa sausage, cut into cubes (use just I meat or a mixture—the more variety, the better the taste)
I	pound mushrooms
3	tomatoes
I	tablespoon tomato puree
	Salt and pepper, to taste
	Sugar
	Some red wine
	(it will greatly improve the flavor)

Bring I cup water to boil in heavy large Dutch oven.
Add sauerkraut and cabbage, cook until soft.

Heat oil in a large skillet. Add onion and meat, cook until browned. Remove from skillet and add to cabbage mixture. Add remaining ingredients and cook I hour. Serve with bread or potatoes.

Please note: The quantity of each ingredient is very flexible and you can experiment with different combinations, but remember that the cabbage is the most important and the healthiest part of the Bigos. Be Adventurous!!

6 to 8 Servings

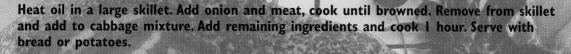

THE BEACH BOYS

Bruce Johnston's
Surf-Potato

My wife, Harriet, gave me a lot of help with this recipe.

1	potato, baked
1	tablespoon olive oil
1	package firm tofu
1	veggie burger, cut into bite-size cubes
1	cup carrots, sliced and steamed
1	cup mushrooms, sliced
2	tablespoons light Italian salad dressing
	Salt and pepper, to taste

Heat oil in large skillet. Add tofu, veggie burger, carrots and mushrooms. Slice open potato and sprinkle with salad dressing. Top with skillet mixture. Season with salt and pepper and serve.

2 Servings

Veggie-Burger

2	cups cooked chickpeas
3/4	cup ground sesame seeds
3/4	cup fresh parsley
2	eggs, beaten
2	tablespoons flour
2	stalks celery, chopped
3	large garlic cloves, minced
1	tablespoon soy sauce
1	tablespoon fresh basil, chopped
1	teaspoon Worcestershire sauce
	Salt and pepper, to taste

Mash chickpeas with fork until smooth. Add remaining ingredients one at a time until well blended. Refrigerate overnight.

Form mixture into 6 burger-size patties. Heat small amount of olive oil in large nonstick skillet. Cook until both sides are browned and patties are cooked through.

6 Servings

BEE GEES

Sunday Morning Heaver From Robin Gibb's Kitchen

I	tablespoon vegetable oil
4	ounces tempeh (cultured beancake), sliced into thirds
I	tablespoon soy sauce
2	slices bread, lightly toasted
I	tablespoon mustard
	Mayonnaise spread
	Alfalfa sprouts
I	tomato, sliced
I	small red onion, sliced thin

Heat oil in large nonstick skillet. Sprinkle tempeh slices with soy sauce and place in skillet. Cook each side 6 minutes.

Spread mustard on I slice bread, spread remaining slice with mayonnaise. Top I slice with tempeh, alfalfa sprouts, tomato and onion. Cover with remaining bread slice.

Enjoy with a glass of carrot juice.

I Serving

TONY BENNETT

Anna Benedetto's Lasagna

I helped my mother (Anna Benedetto) by staying out of the kitchen. She was a fantastic lady from Calabria, a region of southern Italy. My favorite recipe was her lasagna. The secret of her cooking: it was light.

Today, I keep in good singing form by eating well, staying healthy, and drinking good water.

1 1/4	pounds ground beef
2	medium onions, chopped
1/2	pound hot Italian sausage
5 to 6	garlic cloves, minced
1	28-ounce can Italian plum tomatoes
1	28-ounce can Italian puree
2	6-ounce cans tomato paste
1/4	cup minced fresh basil
1/4	teaspoon cinnamon
1	teaspoon salt
1/2	teaspoon freshly ground black pepper
1	pound lasagna noodles, cooked *al dente*
2	16-ounce containers ricotta cheese
3	eggs, lightly beaten
1/2	pound Pecorino Romano cheese, grated

Preheat oven to 350° F.

Brown ground beef and onions together; drain fat. Set aside. Remove sausage from casing; crumble and place in large pot with garlic, cook briefly. Add tomatoes, tomato puree, and tomato paste. Season with basil, cinnamon, salt, and pepper. Add ground beef mixture and stir well. Simmer sauce for 20 minutes, stirring occasionally. Combine ricotta and eggs in bowl.

In 15-inch lasagna pan, place small amount of sauce on bottom; layer with 1/4 noodles, 1/3 ricotta mixture, 1/3 grated cheese; cover with 1/4 sauce. Repeat layers twice. Top with remaining noodles, and cover with remaining sauce.

Bake 45 minutes. Let sit 10 minutes before serving. Buon' Appetito.

6 to 8 Servings

Tony Bennett

Clint Black & Roy Rogers

Clint's Guiltless Burritos

8   corn tortillas
4   boneless, skinless chicken breasts, broiled or baked,
    shredded
1/2 cup shredded lettuce
1/2 cup diced tomato
    Salsa
    Fat free spicy black bean dip
    Fat free sour cream

Preheat oven to 350°F.

Wrap tortillas in foil and place in oven 5 minutes.
Remove from oven; fill each tortilla with equal
amounts of ingredients and roll up.

8 servings

Roy Rogers' Chicken & Dumplings

This is my favorite recipe!

Chicken
1   2 1/2-pound roasting chicken
Garlic salt, onion salt, celery salt,
paprika, and pepper, to taste.

Dumplings
1 1/2 cups flour
2   teaspoons baking powder
1/2 teaspoon salt
3   tablespoons shortening
3/4 cup milk

For chicken:
Place chicken in heavy large Dutch oven. Cover
with water. Bring to boil. Reduce heat, add
seasonings. Cook until meat pulls away from
bones easily. Remove chicken from pot. Remove
and discard bones. Return meat to pot.

For dumplings:
Sift together flour, baking soda and salt. Using fork or pastry cutter, cut in shortening.
Mix in milk. Drop by spoonfuls into chicken soup. Cook uncovered 10 minutes. Cover and
cook 10 minutes. Ladle soup and dumplings into bowls. Serve.

4 Servings

The Blues Brothers
Elwood Blues
Dan Aykroyd

Chicken Sandwich

I	(6-ounce) boneless, skinless chicken breast
	Louisiana Spice Mix
I	tablespoon butter or margarine
I	onion roll, split and toasted
	Chili-Garlic Mayonnaise
I	leaf lettuce
I	large tomato, sliced
2	tablespoons sour cream
	pickled jalapeño slices
	Tabasco® pepper sauce

Sprinkle chicken breast generously with spice mix. In small skillet, melt butter over medium-high heat and add chicken. Cook about 3 minutes on each side or until nicely browned. Spread roll with Chili-Garlic Mayonnaise on each side. Place chicken on bottom half of roll; top with lettuce, tomato, sour cream, jalapeño, and Tabasco sauce and then top half of roll.

Makes I serving

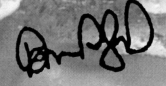

Louisiana Spice Mix

2 1/2	tablespoons	salt
2 1/2	tablespoons	paprika
2	tablespoons	garlic powder
I 1/2	tablespoons	onion powder
I	tablespoon	cayenne pepper
I	tablespoon	dried oregano
I	tablespoon	dried thyme
2	tablespoons	coarse black pepper
I 1/2	teaspoons	white pepper

Combine all ingredients in a jar and shake till well mixed. Makes about I cup.

Chili-Garlic Mayonnaise

I	cup	mayonnaise
I	tablespoon	chili garlic paste (see note)
1/2	teaspoon	Jamaican jerk seasoning (see note)
3	large	cloves garlic, pressed

Combine all ingredients in a small bowl and mix well.

NOTE: Chili garlic paste is available in Oriental food shops and other food specialty stores. Jamaican jerk seasoning is also available in food specialty stores, but if you can't find it, try the following mixture: I teaspoon ground allspice, I teaspoon ground thyme, I teaspoon garlic powder, I teaspoon sugar, 1/2 teaspoon cayenne pepper, 1/2 teaspoon black pepper, 1/2 teaspoon ground nutmeg, and 1/2 teaspoon ground cinnamon.

Boyz II Men

Our Favorite Banana Pudding

We spent days figuring out what we all loved and wanted to contribute. This is the favorite food among all of us boyz.

This is the boyz, version.

4   cups cold milk
1   3.9-ounce package vanilla or chocolate instant pudding mix
1   teaspoon banana extract
6   bananas, sliced

Pour milk into large bowl, add pudding mix and banana extract. Beat with whisk or electric mixer on low speed, 2 minutes. Pour 1/2 of pudding mixture into large serving bowl. Layer bananas over pudding, pour remaining pudding mixture over bananas. Layer remaining banana on top and cover with plastic wrap. Refrigerate. Serve cold.

Makes enough for all of us BOYZ!

BON JOVI

David Bryan's Famous Grilled Whole Maine Moon Lobster

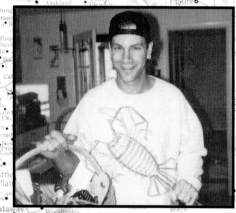

2	Maine lobsters
1	lemon, cut in half
1	head garlic, peeled, minced
1	teaspoon Old Bay® seasoning
1	teaspoon oregano
	Cracked pepper
	Fresh parsley, minced

Slice lobsters down center of belly, do not cut through shell. Clean and rinse lobsters thoroughly. Place towel over claws and hit with wooden mallet.
Squeeze lemon over lobster. Mix together garlic, Old Bay seasoning, oregano and pepper; spread evenly over lobsters. Wrap lobsters in foil and place, back-side down, on a preheated barbecue grill. Cook 5 minutes, turn and cook additional 5 minutes.

Open a bottle of wine, light candles and enjoy the feast!

2 Servings

Tico Torres' Dishwasher Salmon

This unconventional means of cooking fish came quite by accident while we were in Vancouver recording our album, *Slippery When Wet.* This is one of the greatest ways I know to make perfectly steamed fish.

Dishwasher Salmon

1	large salmon, scaled and cleaned
	Juice of large lemon
1/4	cup fresh parsley, minced
1/8	cup mixture dill, salt and pepper
2	large pieces foil
1	large lemon, sliced
4	sprigs parsley, whole

Marinate fish in lemon juice, minced parsley and dill mixture. Wrap fish in foil tightly. Place on top rack of dishwasher; cook, using one wash cycle and one dry cycle. Unwrap fish and garnish with lemon slices and parsley sprigs.

Note: This unconventional means of cooking fish came quite by accident while we were in Vancouver recording our album Slippery When Wet. We took a break and did some fishing for the evening's meal. When we returned, I prepped the salmon and then realized that there wasn't a stove to cook it in. Improvising with a dishwasher turned out to be a great discovery. Since then, it's one of the greatest ways I know to make perfectly steamed fish.

6 Servings

BON JOVI

Richie Sambora's

My Favorite! Chicken from Hell! Olive Tapenade Chicken with Angel-Hair Pasta and Olive Marinara

This is my all time favorite recipe, which Chef Andy Ennis has prepared for Cher, Rosanne, myself, and many others. This recipe has been infamously renamed "Chicken from Hell", because it's so amazing it's sinful!

Sauce
1/4	cup olive oil
3	onions, chopped
1	head garlic, minced
2	28-ounce cans whole tomatoes, chopped
1	28-ounce can tomato puree
1/2	cup cured black olives, pitted, chopped coarsely
1	bay leaf
1	tablespoon basil
1	teaspoon oregano
1	teaspoon cayenne
1	teaspoon sugar
1/4	teaspoon salt

Tapenade
1/2	cup cured black olives, pitted
2	tablespoons capers
6	garlic cloves, minced
6	anchovy fillets, minced (optional)
3	tablespoons lemon juice
1/4	cup olive oil
12	boneless chicken breasts, rinsed, patted dry
3	cups bread crumbs
1/2	cup parsley, chopped
1/2	teaspoon freshly ground black pepper
1-1/2	pounds angelhair pasta, cooked

For sauce:
Heat oil in heavy large pot. Add onions and garlic, cook 8 minutes. Add tomatoes, puree, seasonings and sugar. Bring to boil, reduce heat. Let simmer 1 hour. Stir occasionally.

For tapenade:
Using food processor, mix together olives, capers, garlic and anchovies. Add lemon juice. Gradually add oil until thick paste is formed.

Preheat oven to 425°F.

Rub each chicken breast with tapenade. In separate bowl, combine bread crumbs, parsley and pepper. Coat each chicken breast with bread crumb mixture. Place on nonstick baking sheet. Bake 10-12 minutes. Add remaining tapenade to sauce.

To serve, slice chicken at an angle, into 4-5 strips. Place small amount of pasta on each plate, ladle generous amount of sauce over pasta. Fan chicken slices over pasta. *Voila!* Serve this with asparagus or grilled vegetables on the side and it makes a colorful dish. Enjoy.

Thanks Andy for the recipe!!!

10-12 Servings

21

TONI BRAXTON

This is the best recipe for tofu cheesecake and it's healthy and tastes great! This recipe would not have been possible without my infamous sous chef, Bert Padell.

TOFU CHEESECAKE

Crust

1	16-ounce box graham crackers, crushed
4	tablespoons sugar
1/2	teaspoon cinnamon
4	tablespoons butter, melted

9 or 10" Spring Form pan
waterbath baking sheet

Filling

2	pounds tofu
2	cups sugar
1 1/2	cups nonfat fruit yogurt
1	teaspoon vanilla
3	tablespoons flour
	Pinch of salt
4	egg whites

Preheat to oven to 400ºF.

Crust: Combine graham cracker crumbs, sugar, cinnamon and butter. Press 1/2 crumb mixture onto sides and bottom on springform pan. Reserve remaining crumb mixture.

Filling: Using electric mixer, beat tofu until creamy. Add sugar, yogurt and vanilla. Sift flour and salt into mixture. In seperate bowl, beat egg whites until soft peaks begin to form. Fold egg whites into tofu mixture. Pour into crust and top with remaining crumb mixture. Place on waterbath baking sheet. Bake 30 minutes. Reduce temperature to 300F and bake 1 1/2 hours.

8 servings

The Real Thing CheeseCake

2	box Zwieback, crumbled
4	tablespoons sugar
4	tablespoons melted butter
1/2	teaspoon cinnamon

9 or 10" Spring Form pan
waterbath baking sheet

3	tablespoons flour
2	cups sugar
2	pounds cream cheese
4	eggs, room temperature
1 1/2	cups sour cream
1	teaspoon vanilla
	pinch of salt

Crust: Combine Zieback and sugar. Mix butter and cinnamon and half to the crumb mixture. The other half use to butter the sides and bottom of pan. Press the crumb mixture onto the sides and bottom of the pan. Make sure the crust is even. Chill.

Cheesecake: Preheat the oven to 400 degrees. Sift together flour, salt and sugar. Add the cream cheese and mix. Beat egg yolks and add to cheese. Add sour cream and vanilla. In a seperate bowl beat egg whites till stiff gradually adding 3 tablespoons of sugar. Fold into the cheese mixture. Pour into crust. Place on the waterbath baking sheet. Bake 1/2 hour at 400 degrees and then 1 1/2 hours at 300 degrees.

8 Servings

Best wishes
Toni Braxton

David Byrne

Leftovers

Leftovers...most of what I cook are leftovers. Leftovers from dinners at home, leftovers from take-out and doggie bags from restaurants. And since there's usually not whole meals left, just side orders or half eaten dishes, I've learned to mix and match.

I usually use a large stainless steel steamer...the kind one can get in your local Chinatown housewares store...you put an inch or so of water in the bottom one and top levels have holes in the bottom, so they fill with steam...quite quickly too...for example, it's faster than a toaster oven for heating or re-heating food.

I don't put the food naked into the steamer, as one usually does in the smaller wooden ones, but I keep the food separated in small bowls...like Japanese or Chinese rice bowls...although sometimes I use one large bowl, like the kind used for Chinese or Japanese noodle dishes, and lay a few different leftovers around on top of a bed of rice (there's always leftover rice).

I often mix nationalities. Leftover mashed potatoes with dal over them instead of gravy. Leftover fish in marinara sauce steamed and rolled up in a tortilla. Leftover veggies over Japanese rice. Chinese broccoli with garlic over left-over noodles. Italian broccoli rabe and brown rice rolled up in a whole wheat chappati.

Sometimes it sounds disgusting, but it usually tastes great...I love strong tastes...so I throw on the garlic sauces, the curries and salsas...let'em steam and soak into the food...and the combinations of flavors and textures sometimes results in a rare treat, better than those found in many hoity restaurants. It's kind of post-modern eating, I guess, although I sort of hate that word.

A TIP-if your leftovers are usually sandwiches, burgers, fries, or fried chicken, forget it. They all get soggy in a steamer and dry in a toaster oven and weird in a microwave (I don't have a microwave of my own, but on a modern tour bus for breakfast the thing gets stuffed with catering from the night before).

Yours Truly,

Johnny Cash

Johnny, a seasoned chili cook, never measures his ingredients. He encourages you to do the same to create your own unique version. Taste the mixture each time you add something.

Johnny's "Old Iron Pot" Family-Style Chili

5	pounds sirloin steak, cut into cubes
	Onions, chopped
	Chili peppers, diced
3	packages chili seasoning mix
	Mexene® chili powder
	Chili Con Carne seasoning mix
	Cumin
	Thyme
	Sage

4	15-ounce cans kidney beans
4	16-ounce cans whole tomatoes
1	6-ounce can tomato paste
	Garlic powder
	Onion powder
2	tablespoons sugar
	Salt

Heat heavy large Dutch oven. Add meat and cook until browned on all sides. Add onions and chili peppers, cook 2 minutes. Add chili seasoning mixes, cumin, thyme and sage. Add beans, tomatoes, tomato paste, garlic and onion powders, sugar and salt. If chili seems too thick, add water. Simmer over low heat 20 minutes. Serve with soda crackers and cold cola. This will serve 12 people, three helpings each!!!

Notes from Johnny:

This chili will be better the next day if stored properly overnight. I have also been known to substitute things, such as snake meat, for the steak. This recipe is taken from the cookbook entitled Recipes and Memories from Mama Cash's Kitchen, a collection of recipes passed down over the last 70 years.

6 to 8 Servings

Johnny Cash

June Carter Cash

Tomato Gravy

1	12-ounce can tomatoes
2	tablespoons vegetable oil
2	tablespoons sugar
	Salt and pepper, to taste
2	tablespoons flour
2	cups of milk

Combine tomatoes, oil, sugar, salt and pepper in skillet over medium heat. Cook about 15 minutes. Mix together the flour and milk, then add to skillet. Cook over medium until mixture thickens. Spoon over hot biscuits.

June Carter Cash

24

CHER

Cher's Tuna Pasta

1/2	pound shell pasta, cooked and drained
1/3	cup mayonnaise, low-fat or regular
2	medium tomatoes, peeled, seeded, and chopped
2	stalks celery, minced
1	can black olives, sliced
3	tablespoons parsley, minced
12	ounces white tuna, drained
	Salt and black pepper, to taste
	Beau Monde® seasoning, to taste

To peel tomatoes, remove stem and with sharp knife make an X on the bottom of each tomato, just deep enough to cut the skin. Place the tomatoes in boiling water for 1 minute or less. Remove, dip under cold water and peel.

in large bowl, mix together pasta and mayonnaise until thoroughly mixed. Add tomatoes, celery, olives, parsley and tuna. Season with salt, pepper and Beau Monde. Serve cold.

I love this cold pasta dish at a summer picnic or barbecue.

4 Servings

THE CHIEFTAINS

Paddy Moloney's Original Irish stew

I make this stew with leftover roasted lamb, but it can also be made with fresh lamb. This is a traditional dish we make in our home in Ireland. My recipe is the favorite of all The Chieftains.

1	tablespoon olive oil
2	pounds roasted lamb, diced; or, 8 lamb cutlets, cut into cubes
2	large onions
4	cups stock
4	carrots, sliced
1	ounce barley
4	whole leeks, sliced
3	pounds potatoes, peeled, cut into thick slices
	Pinch of thyme
	Salt and pepper, to taste
	Fresh parsley, minced

Heat the oil in heavy large Dutch oven. Add lamb and onions, sauté for 5 minutes, add stock, carrots and barley. Bring to a boil, reduce heat and let simmer 45 minutes. Add leeks and potatoes. Bring to boil, adding more liquid if necessary. Cook until potatoes are tender. Season with salt, pepper and thyme. Garnish with fresh parsley and serve.

8 Servings

Paddy Moloney

COMMISSIONED

Fred Hammond's Seafood Gumbreanna named for daughter BreeAnna

2	19-ounce cans bean and ham soup
1	10³/₄-ounce can chicken gumbo soup
1	15-ounce can dark red kidney beans
1	pound Polish sausage, cut into 2-inch wedges
1	tablespoon butter
2	cups frozen okra, defrosted, drained, liquid reserved
2	cups fresh mushrooms, sliced
1	teaspoon seafood seasoning
2	tablespoons Tabasco® pepper sauce
1	teaspoon seasoned salt
1	teaspoon garlic salt
1	teaspoon onion powder
	Pepper, to taste
3	cups cooked rice
1	pound shrimp, peeled, deveined

Place soups and kidney beans in heavy large Dutch oven, bring to boil. Add sausage. Continue cooking.

Melt butter in large skillet; add okra, mushrooms, seafood seasoning, Tabasco, seasoned salt, garlic salt, onion powder and pepper. Cook 15 minutes.

Add skillet mixture to soup mixture. Add rice and shrimp; cover and cook over high heat 20 minutes. Serve with corn bread.

COOLIO

Coolio's Boneless Bird

1	4-pound boneless turkey breast
2	tablespoons olive oil
8	garlic cloves, minced
3	tablespoons rosemary
1	tablespoon paprika
1	tablespoon kosher salt
	Fresh rosemary

Mix together oil, garlic, rosemary, paprika and salt. Rub mixture over turkey and broil or grill 20 minutes each side. Garnish with rosemary.

AKA COOLIO

4 Servings

Crash Test Dummies

Pumpkin Cheesecake

Crust

1 1/2	cups graham cracker crumbs
1/4	cup sugar
6	tablespoons butter, melted

Filling

3	8-ounce packages cream cheese, room temperature
3/4	cup brown sugar
3/4	cup granulated sugar
5	eggs
1	16-ounce can pumpkin
1/2	cup heavy whipping cream
1	teaspoon cinnamon
1/2	teaspoon ground cloves
1/2	teaspoon nutmeg

Topping

3/4	cup brown sugar
6	tablespoons butter
1 1/2	cups chopped pecans

Preheat oven to 350°F.

For crust: Using fork or food processor, mix graham cracker crumbs with sugar. Gradually add butter until mixture sticks together. Press against bottom and sides of 9-inch-diameter springform pan. Chill.

For topping: Mix together sugar and butter until mixture resembles coarse meal. Stir in pecans. Set aside.

For filling: Beat cream cheese with electric mixer on low speed until creamy. Add sugars, continue mixing. Beat in eggs 1 at a time, beating well after each addition, and mix until fluffy. Add remaining ingredients, blend well. Pour into chilled crust. Bake 1 1/2 hours or until center is firm. Remove from oven and sprinkle topping evenly over top; bake additional 15 minutes. Cool on rack. Refrigerate overnight.

8 Servings

Mmm Mmm Mmm!

Bo Diddley
Bo's Egg Custard Pie

¹/₂ cup (1 stick) butter
2 cups of sugar
6 eggs
1 teaspoon vanilla
2 cups milk
   Nutmeg, to taste

Preheat oven to 350°F. Butter bottoms and sides of two 8-inch deep-dish pie pans.

Beat together butter and sugar. Add eggs 1 at a time, beating well after each addition. Add vanilla, milk and nutmeg. Pour equal amounts into pie pans. Bake until top is brown and center is set, about 1 hour. Let cool. Serve.

12 Servings

Heavy D.
Hominy

12 cups water
3 cups hominy corn
3 teaspoons salt
2 teaspoons grated nutmeg
2 teaspoons vanilla extract
2 teaspoons cinnamon
1 8-ounce can condensed milk

Pour water into medium-size pressure cooker. Add hominy corn, cook 1 hour over medium heat. Remove from stove and run cold water over pot 5 minutes to decrease pressure before removing lid. Open and place over low heat. Stir in remaining ingredients. Simmer, uncovered, 15 to 20 minutes. Serve.

6 Servings

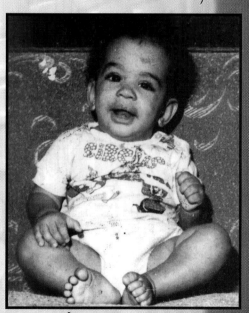

Little Heavy D. at age 2

TRISCUIT QUESADILLAS

Makes 12 appetizers

6 ounces Monterey Jack cheese slices, cut into 12 pieces
24 TRISCUIT Wafers
3 Tablespoons **ORTEGA** Diced Green Chiles
1 Tablespoon **FLEISCHMANN'S** Margarine
½ teaspoon chili powder
1 (12-ounce) jar **ORTEGA** Thick and Chunky Salsa

Place cheese pieces on 12 wafers; top each with ¼ teaspoon chiles and a remaining wafer to form sandwich.

In large non stick skillet, over medium heat, melt half the margarine. Add sandwiches; cook for 5 minutes. Add remaining margarine and turn sandwiches over; cook 5 minutes more or until wafers are toasted and cheese melts. Remove from skillet; sprinkle with chili powder. Serve warm with salsa for dipping.

CHARLIE DANIELS

Charlie's Diet Chili

1	pound lean ground beef
1	medium onion, chopped
2	16-ounce cans undrained tomatoes
1	15-ounce can undrained kidney beans
2	cups celery, sliced
1/2	cup green bell pepper, chopped
1/2	teaspoon garlic salt
	Chili powder, to taste
	Salt, to taste
1	bay leaf

Heat heavy large Dutch oven over medium heat; add ground beef and onion and cook until mixture begins to brown. Pour off all fat and liquid from pot and discard.

Add tomatoes, kidney beans, celery and bell pepper; mix well. Season with chili powder and salt. Add bay leaf, bring mixture to boil; reduce heat. Cover and simmer 1 to 2 hours. Remove bay leaf. Serve hot.

8 Servings

BILLY RAY CYRUS

Steak in a Brown Bag

1	2 1/2 -inch-thick sirloin strip steak
2	tablespoons garlic spread
2	tablespoons vegetable oil
2	teaspoons seasoned pepper
1	teaspoon seasoned salt
1	cup dry bread crumbs

Preheat oven to 375°F.

Rinse steak and pat dry. Mix together garlic spread, oil, salt and pepper. Spread garlic mixture evenly over sides of steak. Press bread crumbs firmly onto garlic spread. Place steak in brown paper bag, close with skewer. Bake 45 minutes for rare.

Billy and his daughter

3 to 4 Servings

DIAMOND RIO

Gene Johnson's Chicken Breasts in Lemon-Caper Sauce

Since Roman times, capers have been a basic ingredient in Italy's and Nashville's favorite sauces.

4	boneless chicken breast halves, skin removed
1/2	cup flour
1/4	cup butter
1	garlic clove, minced
1	cup dry white wine
2	tablespoons lemon juice
1/2	teaspoon pepper
1	tablespoon capers, drained

Cut each chicken breast in half, horizontally. Coat each chicken piece evenly with flour. Melt butter in large skillet over medium heat. Add garlic. Place chicken in skillet, cook until golden brown, about 4 to 6 minutes, each side. Add wine and lemon juice to skillet. Season with pepper. Bring liquid to boil, reduce heat. Add capers and serve.

4 Servings

Dan Truman's Favorite Banana Cake

1 1/2	cups sugar
1/2	cup vegetable oil
3	eggs
1	teaspoon vanilla
1	cup buttermilk
1	cup mashed bananas (2 to 3 bananas)
2	cups all-purpose flour
1	teaspoon baking powder
1	teaspoon baking soda
1	cup walnuts (optional)

Preheat oven to 375°F. Lightly grease and flour 13x9x2-inch cake pan.

Using electric mixer, beat sugar and oil together. Add eggs 1 at a time, beating well after each addition. Add vanilla, buttermilk and mashed bananas. Sift flour, baking powder and baking soda into sugar and oil mixture. Stir in walnuts.

Pour batter into prepared pan and bake 30 to 40 minutes or until toothpick inserted into center comes out clean. Let cake cool. Sprinkle top with powdered sugar and serve.

DIAMOND RIO

Dana Williams' Chocolate Cherry Roadblock

Crust
1	cup all-purpose flour
1 1/2	cups chopped pecans
1/4	cup sugar
1/2	cup (1 stick) butter

Filling
1	8-ounce package cream cheese, room temperature
1	cup powdered sugar
2	8-ounce containers nondairy whipped topping
1	3.9-ounce package instant chocolate pudding mix
3	cups milk
2	17-ounce cans cherry pie filling
1/2	cup toasted pecans, chopped

For crust:
Mix together flour, pecans and sugar. Using fork or pastry cutter, blend in butter until mixture holds together. Press crust onto bottom and sides of 9-inch-diameter pie pan.

For filling:
Using electric mixer, blend together cream cheese, powdered sugar, 1 container whipped topping. Spread evenly into crust. Mix together pudding mix with milk. Spread over first layer. Top with remaining whipped topping. Pour pie filling over topping; do not mix with whipped topping. Sprinkle top with toasted pecans. Chill 2 to 3 hours. Serve.

15 to 20 Servings

Marty's Spaghetti-o!!!

He makes it very simple-take 2 cans of Ragu®, 1 teaspoon of Cinnamon, 2 teaspoons of brown sugar, brown 1 Lb. of ground turkey. Mesh together and pour over noodles of choice. Very Simple....

Placido Domingo
Mocha Tarte de la noche

This is the best dessert late night, listening to classical music sitting by the fire.

Crust

1	square unsweetened chocolate, finely ground
3/4	cup walnuts, finely chopped
3/4	cup unsifted flour
1/4	cup light brown sugar
2	tablespoons sweet butter, chilled and cut into pieces
1	tablespoon cold water
1	teaspoon vanilla

Filling

1/2	cup sweet butter, room temperature
3/4	cup sugar
1	square unsweetened chocolate, melted
2	teaspoons instant espresso coffee
2	large eggs

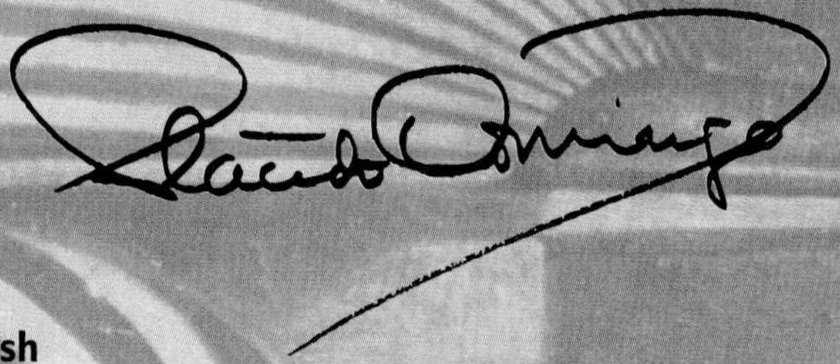

Topping

2	cups heavy whipping cream
2	tablespoons instant espresso coffee
1	cup sifted powdered sugar
	Semi-sweet chocolate shavings for garnish
	Walnut halves for garnish

Preheat oven to 375°F. Grease 9-inch-diameter pie pan.

For crust:

Using food processor, chop chocolate. Add walnuts, continue blending until finely chopped. With processor on, add flour, sugar, chilled butter, water and vanilla, 1 ingredient at a time. Process until mixture forms a ball. Press into prepared pie pan. Bake 15 minutes. Cool on wire rack.

For filling:

Using electric mixer on low speed, beat butter until creamy. Gradually add sugar, melted chocolate and instant coffee. Add eggs 1 at a time, beating well after each addition. Pour filling into completely cooled crust. Cover with plastic wrap and refrigerate 5 to 6 hours before serving.

For topping:

Mix together cream, instant coffee and powdered sugar. Refrigerate in tightly sealed container. Remove from refrigerator, beat with electric mixer or whisk until stiff peaks form. Spread over tart, garnish with chocolate shavings and walnut halves.

8 Servings

Dr. John

New Orleans is the best place for shrimp and music in the country!

Dr. John's Shrimp New Orleans

1 1/2	cups extra virgin olive oil
1/4	cup butter
1	clove garlic, cut in half, do not peel
1	tablespoon Italian dry seasoning mix
1	bay leaf
1	teaspoon seasoned pepper
1	teaspoon cayenne pepper
1	pound (21-25 count per pound) Gulf shrimp with heads, do not peel
1/4	cup white wine
	Salt, to taste
1	loaf French bread, heated

Heat olive oil, butter, garlic, Italian seasoning and bay leaf in large skillet, sauté about 8 minutes, until garlic is soft. Add seasoned pepper and cayenne pepper, sauté 3 minutes. Add shrimp to skillet, cook over low heat 5 minutes, until shrimp turn dark pink. Add wine and season with salt.

Pour shrimp with sauce into serving bowl. Serve with hot bread and Enjoy!

Mac Rebennak
"Dr. John"

2 Servings

MELISSA ETHERIDGE

Red Bean and Rice "Soup"

1	cup dried kidney beans, soaked overnight
2	tablespoons virgin olive oil
2	garlic cloves, minced
1	small onion, finely diced
1	celery stalk, chopped
1	large carrot, grated
1/2	teaspoon dried basil
1/4	teaspoon dried thyme
1	15-ounce can tomatoes, chopped, drained, liquid reserved
1	tablespoon sun-dried tomato puree, or tomato paste
1	bay leaf
	Salt, to taste
1	cup uncooked rice*

Butter or extra-virgin olive oil
Fresh parsley, minced
Freshly ground pepper
Fresh Romano, Parmesan or soy cheese

Heat oil in heavy large Dutch oven. Add garlic, onion, celery, carrot, thyme and basil. Sauté over medium heat until onion becomes soft, about 5 minutes. Add tomatoes, tomato puree or paste and bay leaf. Add water to tomato liquid to yield 8 cups; add to pot.

Drain beans and add to pot. Bring mixture to boil, lower heat and let simmer 40 minutes. Add rice and continue cooking 20 minutes.

Serve "soup" in bowls topped with butter, parsley and a generous amount of pepper. Pass the cheese and a small grater...

* Brown or short-grain white rice can be used. If using brown rice, place in bowl, cover with water and soak 1 hour, drain before adding to pot. Cook 35 minutes.

6 to 8 Servings

FOUR TOPS
DUKE FAKIR

Duke's Pineapple Crayfish and Shrimp Curry

1/4	cup olive oil
1	large onion, chopped
4	garlic cloves
1	pound crayfish tails
1 1/2	pounds shrimp, peeled and washed
1	teaspoon curry powder
1	teaspoon ginger
1	teaspoon cinnamon
1	teaspoon nutmeg
	Dash of each: turmeric, oregano, thyme, salt and ground cumin
1	20-ounce can crushed pineapple

Heat oil in heavy large Dutch oven. Add onion and garlic, sauté until onion becomes soft, about 5 minutes. Add shrimp and crayfish, continue cooking over medium heat 5 minutes. Add seasonings and pineapple, cook 5 to 10 minutes.

Serve over rice. IT'S TOPS!

8 Servings

Peter Gabriel

"I love Italian food and these are a couple of my favorite simple dishes."

Tomato Mozzarella Salad

4   large tomatoes
1   pound fresh buffalo mozzarella, sliced
1   small onion
1   garlic clove, crushed
10   fresh basil leaves
1/4 cup olive oil
     Salt and pepper, to taste

Slice 2 tomatoes, set aside. Cut an X through skin of 2 remaining tomatoes, place in boiling water for 2 minutes. Remove and rinse under cold water. Peel, cut in half, remove seeds. Using food processor, combine onion, garlic and 5 basil leaves, gradually adding oil. Add peeled tomatoes and blend. Season with salt and pepper. Layer tomato slices with mozzarella slices on serving dish. Top with blended tomato mixture. Garnish with remaining basil leaves.

4 Servings

Minestrone Soup

4	tablespoons olive oil		1	cup chopped green beans
4	tablespoons butter		1	cup diced potatoes
1	cup chopped carrots		1	cup chopped broccoli
1	large onion, sliced		1	large zucchini, sliced
1	cup chopped celery		2	garlic cloves, peeled
1	cup chopped leaks		1	cup tomato puree
1	cup chopped cauliflower			Salt and pepper, to taste
8	cups water			

Melt butter in heavy large Dutch oven. Add oil. Add carrots, sauté 2 minutes. Add onion, celery, leeks and cauliflower, sauté 5 minutes. Add water, bring to boil. Reduce heat and let simmer 10 minutes. Add remaining ingredients. Season with salt and pepper. Simmer over low heat 1 hour. Remove garlic cloves before serving.

8 Servings

Always dessert!

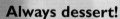

VINCE GILL

Vince's Favorite Rolls

2	cups scalded milk, cooled to 105° to 115°F
1	package active dry yeast
1/4	cup sugar
2	teaspoons salt
1	egg, beaten
1/4	cup melted shortening
5	cups all-purpose flour

Preheat oven to 400°F. Lightly grease 24 muffin-pan cups.

Mix together milk, yeast and sugar. Let sit 10 minutes. Add salt and egg, mix well. Add shortening, mix well. Work in flour. Knead dough until smooth. Cut dough in half; cut each half into 36 equal pieces. Shape each piece into a ball; place 3 balls in each muffin-pan cup. Repeat with remaining dough. Let rise, about 30 minutes until doubled in size. Brush rolls with melted butter and bake 12 to 15 minutes until golden.

Makes about 2 Dozen

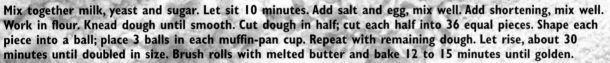

GIPSY KINGS

Salpiquette De Mougette, a Typical Gypsy Recipe

2	pounds of dried Great Northern navy beans, soaked overnight
1	pound fresh pork rind
1	onion, sliced thin
1	pound sausage, crumbled
2	pounds pork, cut into cubes
1	pound lamb, cut into cubes
	Salt and pepper, to taste
	Tabasco® pepper sauce

Place pork rind in heavy large Dutch oven, cover with cold water. Bring to boil, add beans and cook 1 hour. Heat large skillet, add onion, sausage, pork and lamb; sauté until meat is browned. Add meat mixture to beans and simmer 1 to 1 1/2 hours, until beans and meat are tender. Season with salt, pepper and Tabasco sauce.

8 to 12 Servings

This is our favorite recipe on the road prepared by our chef Gene Keenan.

GRATEFUL DEAD

Smoked Corn Chowder

11	ears white corn, shucked, kernels removed and pureed (reserve cobs and some husks)
2	additional ears corn, shucked, kernels removed
1	large potato, peeled and diced (3/8-inch squares)
2	tablespoons roasted garlic puree (about 5 cloves garlic)
1/2	roasted red bell pepper, peeled, seeded and pureed
2	Anaheim chilis, roasted, peeled, seeded and pureed
1	small yellow onion, diced in 3/8-inch squares Salt and pepper, to taste

How to smoke the corn cobs:

There are a number of ways to do this; the easiest is to use a smoker. Assuming you have a smoker; the method would be as follows: Place cobs in smoker and leave for about two or three hours, following manufacturer's instructions, or until the cobs appear to have a thin veil cast over them that is slightly brown in color. They should also have a sweet roasted smell to them. The cobs on the bottom will most likely have become too smoked so discard them or cut the offending material off.

Method for smoking corn cobs with a regular barbecue-like contraption: Place 4 briquettes in the bottom of the grill that have been started in a chimney or on your stove. Don't use lighter fluid lest you take the risk of your cobs tasting like petroleum. Place them on the left or right side so that they not in the center, cover with a couple handfuls of wood chips* that have been soaked in water for 1 hour.

Replace barbecue grate and place corn cobs on top, opposite of the side where the briquettes are. Cover with the lid, dampers open, until there is an impressive amount of smoke. Close dampers and walk a way for 1/2 hour. It may be necessary to add briquettes a number of times. Keep a close eye, when it begins to look like your chips are about halfway burned up add new chips and open up the dampers till the smoke begins to pour out again. Follow above directions for doneness.

Place smoked corn cobs, husks and 8 cups water in heavy large stock pot. Bring to boil. Reduce heat, simmer 1 hour, or until liquid is reduced to half. Remove and discard cobs and husks, strain liquid and return to pot. Add onion, cook at a low boil 5 minutes. Add potatoes and cook until easily pierced with fork, about 15 minutes. Add garlic, peppers and pureed corn, stirring to mix well. Add whole corn kernels and cook until thoroughly heated.

Cooking Notes:
Discard any corn cobs that burn during the smoking process. This recipe is equally delicious made without smoking the corn cobs. If you do this, eliminate making the stock and you will have a soup that can be made in about 30 minutes.This is a great recipe because the pureed corn looks and tastes like sweet cream. The pureed corn can also be the basis for a number of other dishes, particularly crepes and sauces.

* I like to use cottonwood chips, but to my knowledge they are not commercially available. Instead, substitute oak or mesquite, they are readily available and are also yummy.

40

EMMYLOU HARRIS

Emmylou's Crock-Pot® BBQ Chicken

1/2	cup flour
1/2	teaspoon garlic powder
1	teaspoon dry mustard
1	teaspoon salt
1/4	teaspoon pepper
8	chicken thighs
2	tablespoons vegetable oil
1	cup barbecue sauce

Place dry ingredients in a medium paper bag. Shake to mix. Add chicken and shake to coat chicken.

Heat oil in a large skillet. Add chicken to skillet and brown on all sides. Pour 1/2 cup barbecue sauce in Crock-Pot, add chicken and cover with remaining barbecue sauce. Cook on low 6 to 8 hours, covered.

8 Servings

JACKSON BROWNE

My grandmother came to Minneapolis from Norway when she was a young girl, and for many years she was the housemother of a fraternity at the University of Minnesota. Her recipe for Norwegian pancakes comes from a book of handwritten recipes that she passed to my mother, who then gave them to me and my son, Ethan.

Norwegian Pancakes

These are very similar to French crepes, except, they are smaller.

3	eggs
1 1/2	cups milk
1	cup flour
1/2	teaspoon salt

Beat together eggs and milk. Add flour and salt. Mix well. Heat large skillet. Melt small amount of butter in skillet, add enough batter to skillet to make 3-4 pancakes. Cook 1-2 minutes on both sides. Remove from skillet. Stack in warm place until all batter has been cooked.

Serve with powdered sugar, jelly, syrup, a fried egg, or with fruit and yogurt. My favorite is with a little bit of powdered sugar and lemon.

Peanut Butter Swirl Bars

When we all head out from our hometown, Columbia S.C., Soni's mom loads us up with lots of sweets!
Always, these swirls are the first to go!!

1/2	cup chunky peanut butter		1	cup all-purpose flour
1/3	cup butter		1	teaspoon baking powder
3/4	cup packed light-brown sugar		1/4	teaspoon salt
3/4	cup granulated sugar		1	12-ounce package chocolate chips, milk or
2	eggs			semi-sweet
2	teaspoons vanilla extract			

Preheat oven to 350°F. Grease 9 x 13-inch cake pan.
Using electric mixer, beat together peanut butter, butter and sugars. Beat in eggs and vanilla.
Sift in flour, baking powder, salt, and chocolate chips. Stir to mix well. Pour batter into prepared
pan and place in oven 5 minutes. Remove from oven and run knife through batter to marbleize.
Return to oven and bake 25 minutes. Do not over bake.

Soni's Mom's Chili

4	pounds ground beef		1	cup water
1	medium onion, chopped		4	15-ounce cans kidney beans
1	tablespoon chili powder		3	15-ounce cans tomato sauce
1	package chili seasoning mix			Salt, pepper, minced or powdered garlic, dried
				basil, Italian seasoning, all to taste

Heat heavy large Dutch oven. Add ground beef and cook until browned. Add onion, chili powder and chili seasoning mix, cook 5 minutes. Add water, bring to boil, reduce heat and simmer 15 minutes.

Add kidney beans, tomato sauce and remaining seasonings. Cook 1 hour.

These are the basic ingredients I use; all of them can be adjusted to suit your taste. You can use more or
fewer beans, substitute crushed tomatoes for the sauce or even soup. It will never taste the same twice, but
it's always good.

I like it best when it sits overnight and then is heated before serving.

CISSY and WHITNEY HOUSTON

Candied Yams

Ever since I can remember my mom made this dish during the Holidays. To this day the Candied Yams are never forgotten!

4	medium sweet potatoes, boiled, peeled and sliced
1/2	cup (1 stick) butter
2	tablespoons fresh orange juice
1/2	teaspoon lemon juice
1/4	cup honey
1	cup packed brown sugar
1/2	teaspoon cinnamon
1/4	teaspoon nutmeg
	Dash allspice
1/2	teaspoon vanilla

Preheat oven to 375°F.

Layer the sweet potatoes in a medium-size baking dish.

Melt the butter in small saucepan. Add the orange juice, lemon juice, honey, sugars and spices. Cook until thick and syrupy, about 10 minutes. Remove from heat, add vanilla and pour over yams. Bake 30 minutes.

If desired, cool 30 minutes, top with marshmallows and place under broiler until marshmallows are browned.

43

Julio Iglesias

Julio's Paella Valencia

1	small tender chicken
1	thick slice of ham
1	large squid, cut in rings
1 1/2	dozen of clams or mussels, (previously cooked in a little water so that they are open). Don't throw away the remaining broth.
4-6	large shrimp in their shells
1	red snapper fillet, cut into small pieces
14 oz	paella rice (the grains are rounded instead of long) or Arborio rice
8 oz	oil
1	large red pepper, diced
3-4	medium size tomatoes, peeled and diced
1	teaspoon paprika
1	large garlic clove, minced
4	tablespoons of cooked peas
	a couple of saffron threads
1	lemon
	salt
	ground pepper

Once clams or mussels are cooked, remove half of the shell and keep the half with the meat inside for the rice. Cut up a chicken into 8 pieces, dice the ham, and in a large round pan, preferably iron, heat the oil and saute. Once they have a golden color, add the red pepper, the minced garlic and the squid.

Continue slowly cooking and stirring, add more oil if neceesary, add more if necessary, add the diced tomatoes, the paprika and the whole shrimp in it's shell.

Stir very well to insure that everything is evenly cooked, finally add the rice, the peas, the clams or mussels, and the fish.

Add double the volume of water or broth as of rice, don't forget to use the broth left from cooking the clams or mussels and the fish.

Bring to a boil and let boil for a couple of minutes, reduce heat. Add salt if necessary, the ground pepper if you want and the pulverized saffron threads. From now until the paella is finished it should not be stirred.

As the water starts evaporatingg, reduce haet until paella looks dry. Before serving, let stand for a couple of minutes. The paella is served in the pan in which it has been cooked. The lemon should be cut in 4 pieces and set on top of the paella, or served seperately.

Julio

THE JAYHAWKS
Marc Olson's
Otter Tail Chili

1	pound ground beef
1/2	pound pork sausage
1/2	pound bacon
1	large onion, chopped
1	green bell pepper, chopped
1	pound fresh mushrooms, sliced
5	stalks celery, sliced thin
2	16-ounce cans whole tomatoes
3	tablespoons chili powder
1	tablespoons salt
1	tablespoons pepper
4	tablespoon Tabasco® pepper sauce
1	15-ounce can kidney beans
1	15-ounce can pinto beans
	sour cream
	chedder cheese

Heat heavy large Dutch oven. Add ground beef, pork and bacon; cook until beef is browned. Add onion, bell pepper and mushrooms. Sauté 5 minutes. Add tomatoes. Stir in chili powder, salt, pepper and Tabasco sauce; cook 1 hour over low heat. Add kidney and pinto beans, cook 45 minutes. Serve with sour cream and shredded chedder cheese on the side.

6 Servings

VICTORIA WILLIAMS
Momma's Pecan Pie

1/2	cup sugar	1	teaspoon vinegar
3	tablespoons butter, softened	1	tablespoon flour
3	eggs	1	cup whole pecans
3/4	cup maple syrup	1	prepared pie crust, unbaked

Preheat oven to 450°F.

Mix together sugar and butter until smooth. Beat in eggs 1 at a time, beating well after each addition. Stir in syrup and vinegar. Add flour and pecans. Mix well. Pour into pie shell. Bake 10 minutes. Reduce oven temperature to 300°F. Bake 30 minutes.

6 Servings

Grilled Stuffed Portabello Mushrooms

Makes 4 servings

1 cup diced onions
1 teaspoon chopped garlic
2 cups chopped white mushrooms
1 (14 ounce) can artichokes, drained and chopped
¾ cup **SNACKWELL'S** Reduced Fat French Onion
  Snack Crackers, coarsely broken
¼ cup sundried tomatoes, softened in warm water
  for 5 minutes, drained and chopped
2 tablespoons grated Parmesan cheese
¼ teaspoon salt
¼ teaspoon ground black pepper
4 medium to large portabello mushrooms
  (about 1½ pounds), stems removed

In large non stick skillet sprayed with
cooking spray, over medium-high heat,
cook onion and garlic for 2 minutes. Add
chopped mushrooms; cook for
6 to 8 minutes more or until tender.
Remove from heat; stir in artichokes,
crackers, tomatoes, cheese, salt and
pepper. Set aside.

Grill portabello mushrooms, rounded side up for 5 to 6 minutes;
remove from grill. Spoon
cracker mixture onto flat
side of mushrooms,
mounding firmly. Place
stuffed mushrooms on
grill. Cover and cook for
12 to 15 minutes or mushroom is
tender and stuffing is heated through.

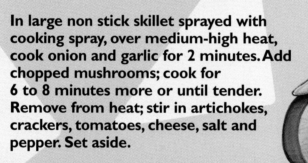

Alan Jackson

When I was young, my mom used to make me this cake on my birthday. Red is my favorite color and cake is one of the best things to eat!

Alan's Favorite Red Velvet Cake

Cake
1½	cups sugar
1½	cups vegetable oil
2	eggs
1	cup buttermilk
1	teaspoon vanilla extract
2½	cups all-purpose flour
1	teaspoon salt
1	teaspoon baking soda
1	tablespoon powdered cocoa
1	teaspoon vinegar
1	1-ounce bottle red food coloring

Frosting
1½	16-ounce boxes of powdered sugar
1½	8-ounce packages cream cheese, room temperature
¾	cup margarine
1	teaspoon vanilla
1½	cups chopped pecans

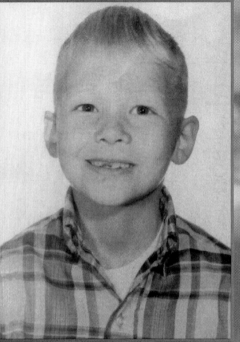

Alan's 1st grade school picture!

For cake:
Preheat oven to 350°F. Lightly grease two 8-inch cake pans. Line bottom of pans with wax or parchment paper.

Using electric mixer, beat together sugar and oil, until well combined. Add eggs 1 at a time, beating well after each addition. Mix in buttermilk and vanilla. Sift in flour, salt, baking soda and cocoa. Add vinegar and food coloring, mix into smooth batter. Pour into prepared pans. Bake 45 minutes or until a toothpick inserted into the center comes out clean. Let cool 15 minutes before removing cakes from pans.

For frosting:
Using electric mixer, beat all ingredients, except nuts, together until smooth. Add nuts. Place 1 cake layer on plate, spread frosting evenly over top. Repeat with remaining layers. Spread remaining frosting evenly over sides of cake. Enjoy!!

6 Servings

B.B. KING

My Favorite German Chocolate Cake

Cake

4	ounces semisweet chocolate
1 1/4	cup (2 1/2 sticks) butter
2	cups sugar
4	eggs, separated
1	teaspoon vanilla
2	cups all-purpose flour
1	teaspoon baking soda
1/2	teaspoon salt
1	cup buttermilk

Coconut-Pecan Frosting

1 1/2	cups evaporated milk
1 1/2	cups sugar
4	egg yolks, slightly beaten
3/4	cups butter
1 1/2	teaspoons vanilla
2	cups coconut
2	cups chopped pecans

Preheat oven to 350° F. Lightly grease three 9-inch pans. Line bottom of pans with wax or parchment paper.

For cake:
Melt chocolate and 1/4 cup of butter in heavy bottom pan. Let cool. Cream together remaining butter and sugar in medium bowl. Beat in egg yolks. Stir in vanilla and chocolate mixture. Sift together dry ingredients. Alternately add dry ingredients and buttermilk to chocolate mixture. Beat egg whites until stiff in large bowl, fold in chocolate mixture. Pour cake batter evenly into the three prepared pans. Bake 30 minutes or until cake springs back. Let cool on racks.

For Frosting:
Combine evaporated milk, sugar, egg yolks, and butter in a saucepan. Add vanilla. Cook over medium heat, stirring continuously until thickened (thick enough to coat back of spoon). Remove from heat. Stir in coconut and pecans. Cool until thick enough to spread over cake. Place 1 cake layer on plate, spread frosting evenly over top. Repeat with remaining layers. Spread remaining frosting evenly over sides of cake. Serve.

8 Servings

Gladys Knight

Gladys' Vegetable Casserole

2	tablespoons butter
1	large onion, chopped
1	bell pepper, chopped
1	bunch broccoli, chopped
1	head cauliflower, chopped
1	cup corn
1	cup green beans
1/2	cup water chestnuts
1	teaspoon garlic powder
1	teaspoon dill
	Salt and pepper, to taste
4	cups ricotta cheese
2	16-ounce containers nonfat cottage cheese
1	cup grated cheddar cheese
1	cup grated mozzarella cheese
1	cup grated Monterey jack cheese
3	slices bread, toasted
	Paprika

Preheat oven to 350°F. Lightly grease large casserole dish.

Melt butter in large skillet. Add vegetables and sauté until onion becomes soft. Season with garlic powder, dill, salt and pepper. Combine cheddar, mozzarella and Monteroy Jack cheeses in medium bowl. Layer 1/4 vegetables in prepared casserole dish, cover with 1/2 ricotta and 1/2 nonfat cottage cheese. Layer 1/4 vegetables over cottage cheese and cover with 1/2 grated cheese. Repeat layering until all ingredients are used, reserving small portion of grated cheese. Crumble toast over top layer and cover with remaining grated cheese. Cook 45 minutes. Sprinkle with paprika for color.

8 to 10 Servings

With Love!
Gladys Knight

LEMON BARS

Makes 16 bars

30 RITZ Crackers, finely rolled (about 1¼ cups crumbs)
½ cup all-purpose flour
1 cup sugar
¼ cup **FLEISCHMANN'S** Margarine, softened
2 eggs
⅓ cup lemon juice
2 teaspoons grated lemon peel
½ teaspoon baking powder
Confectioners' sugar

Mix cracker crumbs, ¼ cup flour and ¼ cup sugar; cut in margarine until crumbly. Press on bottom of greased 9 x 9 x 2-inch square baking pan. Bake at 350° for 10 to 12 minutes; cool at least 10 minutes.

With electric mixer, beat eggs and remaining sugar until foamy, about 1 minute. Blend in lemon juice and peel. Stir in remaining flour and baking powder. Pour over prepared crust. Bake for 12 to 15 minutes more or until set. Cool completely; cut into bars. Sprinkle with confectioners' sugar.

KOOL AND THE GANG

Sir Earl Toon's Grandma's Swordfish Steaks

1	tablespoon basil
4	6-ounce swordfish steaks, 1/2 inch thick
2	teaspoons light olive oil
1/2	cup white wine
2	tablespoons lemon juice
2	tablespoons orange juice
2	tablespoons vinegar
1	tablespoon chopped parsley
1/2	tablespoon mustard
1/4	teaspoon salt
1/4	teaspoon freshly ground pepper
	Pinch cinnamon
	Pinch tarragon
	Pinch cayenne pepper
1/4	cup thinly sliced scallions
1/4	cup mushrooms, chopped
1	Lemon, sliced
	Capers

Preheat broiler. Brush both sides of each swordfish steak with olive oil. Combine remaining ingredients in a small bowl. Spoon mixture over top of each steak. Place under broiler 4 inches from heat, cook about 3 minutes. Turn fish, top with remaining wine mixture. Broil until cooked through, about 3 minutes. Garnish with lemon slices and capers.
4 Servings

Craig Mack

Mack-A-Licious Phat French Toast

2	eggs
2	tablespoons of half-and-half
1	teaspoon flour
1/2	teaspoon nutmeg
1/2	cup (1 stick) butter
4	slices bread
	Cinnamon, to taste

Beat together eggs and half and half. Beat in flour and nutmeg, continue mixing until batter is light and fluffy.

Melt butter in large skillet on low heat. Dip each slice of bread in batter, coat completely. Increase skillet heat to medium and place coated bread in skillet; cook until golden brown. Sprinkle each side with cinnamon.

Mack-A-Licious Phat French Toast, Enjoy!!

4 Servings

KRS-One and Mad Lion

The Festival Roast Fish by KRS-One and Mad Lion
assisted by Pauline Perry

2	medium doctorfish, porgy or grunt
4	stalks calalu
10	small okra
1	medium onion (thinly sliced)
1	small sweet pepper
3	slices Scotch bonnet pepper
	Regular salt
	Black pepper
	Accent salt
	Aluminum foil
	Baking rack

Preheat oven to 400° F. Clean fish thoroughly, making sure the belly is removed, the skin is completely scaled and the fish is split open (the fish market can do this or you can do it yourself). First dice the calalu and the okra together. Mix all the spices, with the calalu, onion, sweet peppers, scotch bonnet peppers and okra to make fish stuffing. Stuff belly of fish. Completely cover fish with aluminum foil and place on baking rack. Bake 45 minutes to 1 hour. Serve with Festival.

Calalu is a green leafy vegetable and and spinach can be a substitute. Scotch bonnet peppers are very hot, you can purchase them dried at most gourmet shops or substitute another type of hot pepper.

Festival

1	cup all-purpose flour
2	tablespoons butter, melted
2	tablespoons baking powder
1	tablespoon granulated sugar
1	cup water (or less)
	Pinch of salt
1	small bowl
1	small pan with hot oil

Combine all ingredients in bowl. Mix together with fingers, adding wter gradually until mixture is soft enough to roll into an eggroll shape. Place in pan and fry until brown on both sides. Serve with Roast fish.

PATTI LABELLE

Patti's Holiday Favorites

These string beans and my real old-fashioned herb and bread stuffing have been favorites of my family for years. I know a lot of folks add things like apples or sausage to their stuffing, but my guys (my three sons and husband) like a simple-style dressing that they can drown in gravy.

String Beans "La Bella"

3	tablespoons vegetable oil		1/4	teaspoon seasoned salt
1	medium onions, chopped		1/8	teaspoon salt
4	garlic cloves, minced		2	cups water
1	15-ounce cans whole peeled tomatoes, chopped		2	pounds green beans
1	6-ounce can tomato paste		1/2	cup grated Mozzarella cheese
1/2	teaspoon dried oregano leaves		1/2	cup grated Provolone cheese

Heat oil in medium saucepan over medium-high heat. Add onions, garlic and green beans; cook and stir until onions are tender. Remove from heat. Mix together whole tomatoes, tomato paste, oregano, salts and water. Layer the bottom of heavy large Dutch oven with generous amount of the tomato mixture. Place layer of green beans on tomato mixture and cover with layer of cheese. Repeat layering until all ingredients are used.

Cook, tightly covered, over medium heat until cheese melts and mixture is heated through.

12 Servings

Old-Fashioned Turkey Stuffing

1/2	cup plus 2 tablespoons (1 1/4 sticks) butter
1	cup celery, finely chopped
1	large green pepper, diced
1	large onion, finely chopped
2	small jalapeños peppers, seeded and finely minced
1/2	teaspoon seasoned salt
1	tablespoon poultry seasoning
1	large loaf of day-old bread or stale bread, crumbled

Melt 2 tablespoons butter in large skillet. Add celery, green pepper, onion and jalapeño: sauté until tender. Season with salt and poultry seasoning. Mix together remaining butter with bread, using hands, until thoroughly mixed. Add water for moisture, if necessary. Add bread mixture to skillet, gently mix bread into vegetable mixture, sauté until heated through.

Stuff that Bird!

6 to 8 Servings

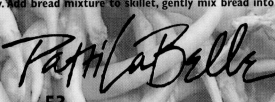

Cyndi Lauper

The first thing I have to tell you is something my friend Gino told me, "Iffa you don'ta gotta da right ingredientsa, it'sa gonna affecta da taste-ah...You gatta getta fresha vegeteh-bles, because-za dat meenza everyting to da taste-ah". So when you go to the store, make sure the little broccoli rob buds aren't in bloom (no yellow flowers!). This will be a big help to the taste and to the presentation, which of course is everything...In fact if we're going in this direction, what the hell, FRESH EVERYTHING!, including the garlic in the bottom drawer of the refrigerator also in bloom. Get rid of it! O.K. Now go shopping.

Broccoli Rob and Pasta for Four

Here's your list:
- 1/4 cup extra-virgin olive oil
- 6 garlic cloves
- 2 good-size bunches fresh broccoli rob (rabe)
- 1/4 teaspoon crushed red pepper flakes (O.K., so this is dried; if you have them and they're not from last year, use what you have) Anchovy paste, to taste. (This is optional. Some people use it to cut the bitter taste but just a drop. Taste it and see what you like.)
- 1 1/2 pounds of your favorite brand of imported Italian pasta (I prefer pasta in a box). Keep in mind that the pasta you buy shouldn't be too big. The broccoli rob will get lost. Something like orchietta or penne is best.

Now, you'll need a BIG pot (it's better to have too much water than too little), a medium-size pot, a cutting board, knife for chopping (like a ginsu), a garlic press, a colander,... oh and some salt and a large spoon.
Fill the BIG pot with some cold, filtered or bottled water and a touch of salt. Put it on the back burner over medium heat (it will eventually boil... pretty great huh?). O.K., leave that and wash the broccoli rob using the colander. When your finished, (my mother would have soaked it for an hour in what she calls a sony... not my record company...and I'm not sure what that is exactly, except that she says it removes the toxins... and she's big on doing that, so I guess she wouldn't start boiling the water right away) cut the ends off the broccoli rob, about 3 inches and throw away. Cut the rest into 1 1/2-inch pieces. Try to use most of the leaves and try not to mess the buds.

Peel 2 to 3 garlic cloves (oh and personally, I never use elephant garlic.. it doesn't have much taste to me).

Put 2 tablespoons olive oil in the medium-size pot and cook on medium heat. When the oil gets hot, press the garlic through the garlic press, let that fall into the pot, (the garlic, not the press). It will sizzle. Reduce the heat to low and add a pinch of red pepper flakes. Now, add broccoli rob. Stir gently with your spoon, cover and cook slowly on low heat. My grandmother always said it should cook in it's own juices (but you could add a tiny bit of pasta water if ya had to...but not yet).

And speaking of pasta, how's that water coming? It should be boiling like crazy. Here comes the big moment. Drop pasta in the water (without the cardboard). Add a little olive oil so that the pasta won't stick. Set the timer for 8 to 10 minutes. (I like it on the Al Dente side, Less is more, Get it? I kill myself sometimes... but seriously folks, taste it and see what you like).
Hey! Keep checking the broccoli rob! It should turn a nice dark color. Don't let it turn light green. That's cooked too much. Maybe you should taste it and see how's it doing. Add a pinch of salt. Taste again. Here 's when you might add anchovy paste, just a drop. Don't make it too salty. Taste it again. If it's done, remove it from the heat till the pasta's ready...O.K.? Now, take a cup of water out of the pasta pot and set it aside.
When the timer rings, or when the pasta is the texture you like, drain and add to the broccoli rob. Toss gently. Remember that cup of pasta water? Add about 1/2 cup, a little at a time, to the broccoli rob. Don't make it too watery. If it's too dry, add a little more water but taste as you go. Toss gently and serve with a tiny plate of crushed red pepper and a little extra olive oil on the side. This dish also goes great with salad...Oh, and hey, *bon appetit.* Here's when you might want to turn on some good accordion music.

TRACY LAWRENCE

Tracy's Arkansas Stew

I	pound cubed beef
4	stalks celery, chopped
I	large onion, chopped
6	carrots, chopped
3	teaspoons salt
3	teaspoons black pepper
I	regular can green peas
1/4	cup flour
2	quarts water
I	can beef stock

Hush Puppies

I	cup yellow cornmeal
1/2	teaspoon salt
1/4	teaspoon pepper
1/4	cup onion, chopped
I	large fresh Jalapeno pepper, seeded, chopped
2/3	cup buttermilk
4	cups vegetable oil

For stew:
Brown beef in skillet. Remove beef. Add flour slowly to grease! Brown flour. Add approximately 1/2 cup of water. Stir flour mixture to prevent lumps. Add flour mixture to large pot. Add browned beef, onion, celery, peas, salt pepper, water and beef broth. Simmer until vegetables and tender.

For hush puppies:
Mix together all ingredients. Drop spoonful of batter into catfish oil. Fry 3 to 4 minutes or until golden, turning once. Place on paper towels to absorb excess oil. Serve hush puppies with catfish.

4 Servings

55

John Paul
JONES
LED
ZEPPELIN

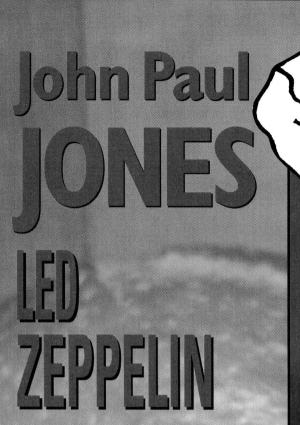

Pa amb Tom a'quet
(pronounced pam toe-mak-et)

This is an utterly delicious, typical Catalan snack from eastern Spain. I first came across it in Barcelona while producing an album for the Catalan Theater company *La Fura Dels Baus*. This is often served during lunch or dinner, although just passing the kitchen in the farmhouse was excuse enough to eat some. Food and music seem to be of equal importance in Spain, a good reason for doing as many projects there as possible.

1   loaf crusty country-style bread, sliced thick
        Garlic cloves
        Plum tomatoes, sliced
        Extra-virgin olive oil

Toast bread slices evenly on both sides. Cut a clove of garlic in half and rub 1 side of each bread slice. Repeat until all slices have been rubbed with garlic. Top with tomato slice. Drizzle with olive oil. You can also top with salt or anchovies.

10 to 12 Servings

Lisa Loeb Sugar Cookies

When I'm in my studio, I don't have time to cook so I decided to include this cookie recipe that my mom gave me. She sends me tins of sugar cookies from Texas to snack on while I work. Not only are they tasty, but they are sparkley and beautiful to look at!

3/4	cup sugar
1	tablespoon plus 1 teaspoon milk
1	teaspoon vanilla
2/3	cup shortening
1	egg
2	cups all-purpose flour
1 1/2	teaspoons baking powder
1/4	teaspoon salt
	colored sugar or sprinkles

Using electric mixer, beat together sugar, milk, vanilla and shortening. Add egg, beat well. Sift flour, baking powder and salt into sugar mixture. Beat on low speed until well blended. Wrap dough in plastic wrap and refrigerate overnight.

Preheat oven to 375°F.

Remove dough from plastic wrap. Place on floured surface. Using a rolling pin, roll dough out to 1/8-inch thickness. Cut into desired shape. Place cut cookies on ungreased nonstick baking sheet. Sprinkle with colored sugar. Repeat until all dough is used.

Bake 4 to 6 minutes. Transfer to racks immediately.

Makes about 2 dozen

Mrs. Loeb can I please order 3 dozen cookies for next Thursday?

"Angelic" Tandoori Chicken Kebabs

2   boneless chicken breasts, trimmed, cut into cubes
Juice of 1 lemon
3/4   cup plain low fat yogurt
1   garlic clove, crushed
1   tablespoon fresh ginger, minced
1/2   teaspoon cumin powder
1/2   teaspoon ground coriander
1/4   teaspoon onion powder
1/4   teaspoon cayenne pepper
Pinch turmeric (for coloring)

Place chicken in medium bowl. Cover with lemon juice, let sit 15 minutes. Mix together remaining ingredients in separate bowl. Pour over chicken and marinate 6 hours in refrigerator.

Place chicken on skewers, brush with marinade. Place skewers on hot grill or under broiler. Cook 10 to 12 minutes, turning occasionally. Kebabs are cooked when chicken juices run clear and marinade becomes crisp. Serve with sautéed onions, saffron rice and lemon wedges.

2 Servings

58

MADONNA

Cholesterol Cherry Torte

This is a recipe that has been in my family for years. The current Ciccone Cherry Torte champion is my sister Melanie. The last time I made it, my brother, Christopher, had to run to my house to 'save the dessert.' He's a master at everything he does. Hate him.

Crust

	cups All-purpose flour
2	cup brown sugar
	cup chopped pecans
	cup butter or margarine, cut into small pieces

Preheat oven to 400°F.

Filling

1	8-ounce package cream cheese
1	cup powdered sugar
2	packages Dream Whip®
1	teaspoon vanilla
1	17-ounce can of cherry pie filling

For crust:
Mix together flour, sugar and pecans. Using fork or pastry cutter, cut in butter, until mixture resembles coarse meal. Firmly pat down in a large baking dish. Bake 15 minutes. Cool, then break apart and respread in the same pan.

For filling:
Using electric mixer, beat together cream cheese and sugar. Add Dream Whip and vanilla. Beat until well mixed. Spread over crust. Dollop each cherry individually onto cream filing about 1 inch apart. Refrigerate several hours before serving.
Servings

Rita Marley

Steamed Whole Fish with Okra, Carrots and Jamaica Crackers

This traditional Jamaican dish is a total meal in one.

Rita's Special Steamed Whole Fish with Okra, Carrots and Jamaican Excelsior Crackers

1	3-pound red snapper, whole, scaled and cleaned
	Juice of 1 lime
1	pound carrots, sliced
2	large onions, chopped
1	dozen okra, sliced
3	garlic cloves, minced
1/4	cup thyme
	Salt and pepper, to taste
1	whole Jamaica scotch bonnet pepper
1	cup water
3	teaspoons butter
2	dozen Jamaica Excelsior crackers*
	Parsley flakes

Place fish in large skillet, rub with lime juice. Mix together carrots, onions, okra, garlic thyme, salt and pepper. Fill inside of fish and cover top with vegetable mixture. Add whole scotch bonnet pepper to skillet for flavor. Add 1/2 cup water to pan, cook over medium heat 10 minutes. Add butter, crackers, remaining water. Cook 10 minutes. Sprinkle with parsley and serve.

4 Servings

* Water crackers can be substituted for Jamaican Excelsior crackers.

Ziggy Marley

Steamed Calaloo with Boiled green Bananas

Ziggy's Basic Meal: Steamed Calaloo* with Boiled Green Bananas

2	bunches calaloo, leaves washed and chopped
1	medium onion, chopped
8	garlic cloves, minced
2	medium tomatoes, diced
2	tablespoons butter
	Salt and pepper, to taste
1	ripe avocado, peeled and sliced
1	large tomato, cut into quarters
1	head lettuce, washed and torn into bite-size pieces

Bananas

5	green bananas
2	tablespoons butter
1	teaspoon salt

Place calaloo in medium-size saucepan, cook over low heat. Add onion, garlic and diced tomatoes. Cook until calaloo begins to turn bright green, about 20 minutes. Add butter. Season with salt and pepper.

Garnish with ripe avocado slices, tomato and lettuce. Add additional garlic, if desired.

For bananas: Cut a lengthwise slice in peel of each banana. Bring 2 cups water to boil in small saucepan. Add bananas, butter and salt. Boil 30 to 45 minutes, until peel begins to pull away from banana easily. Remove bananas from water. Remove peel and mash with a fork or eat whole.

*Calaloo is the Jamaican version of spinach, which may be used as a substitute.

Barbara Mandrell

A recipe that's easy to make on the road.

Shish Ke-Babs

1	5-ounce bottle Worcestershire	3	ribeye steaks, trimmed, cut into cubes
1/2	cup soy sauce	3	bell peppers, diced the same size as steak
2	teaspoons ginger powder	3	onions, diced the same size as steak
	Pepper, to taste	1	20-ounce can chunky pineapple

Mix Worcestershire, soy sauce, ginger powder and pepper in small bowl. Place a piece of steak, bell pepper, onion and pineapple on skewer, repeat until all ingredients are used. Place in 13x9x2-inch baking dish and cover with marinade. Marinate 3 hours, turning periodically. Cook on grill or under broiler, 3 to 5 minutes each side.

6 Servings

Barbara Mandrell

The Marsalis Family

Mrs. Marsalis is the wife of Ellis and the mother of Branford, Wynton, Ellis Jr., Delfeayo, Mboya and Jason. The Marsalis clan hails from New Orleans and this recipe has a uniquely southern flair. It is a family favorite enjoyed at Christmas. From the Marsalis' home to yours, enjoy!

Mrs. Marsalis' Pumpkin Pecan Pie

1 1/2	quarts butter pecan ice cream
1	cup sugar
1	cup canned pumpkin
1	teaspoon cinnamon
1/4	teaspoon ginger
1/4	teaspoon nutmeg
1/4	teaspoon salt

1	cup heavy whipping cream, whipped
1/4	cup packed light-brown sugar
2	tablespoons butter
1	tablespoon water
1/2	cup pecans, chopped

Place one 9-inch deep-dish pie pan in freezer 30 minutes.
(Mrs. Marsalis prefers stainless steel.)
Working quickly, line bottom and sides of frozen pan with ice cream. Be careful to keep ice cream off edge of pan! Freeze at least 2 hours.
Combine sugar, pumpkin, spices and salt in saucepan; cook over low heat 3 minutes. Let cool.
Fold 3/4 cup whipped cream into pumpkin mixture. Spoon pumpkin mixture into frozen ice cream crust. Freeze 2 more hours.
Reserve remaining whipped cream for garnish.
In small saucepan over medium heat, combine brown sugar, butter and water. Bring to boil, cook 1 to 2 minutes. Remove from heat. Stir in pecans. Let cool.
Spoon brown sugar mixture around edge of pie. Fill center with reserved whipped cream. Freeze until set. Refrigerate 10 minutes before serving.

8 to 10 Servings

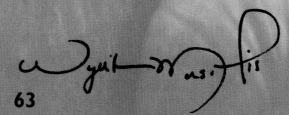

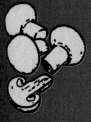

Paul and Linda McCartney

Paul & Linda's Chili Non Carne

The best chili you'll get this side of Tijuana! This is one of our favorite vegetarian recipes. Serve with rice, mashed potatoes or an avocado salad.

Paul and Linda's Chili Non Carne

- 2   tablespoons vegetable oil
- 1   medium onion, chopped
- 1½   level teaspoons chili powder (or more, according to taste)
- 2   4½-ounce packets TVP Chunks* or 4 vegetable burgers, crumbled
- 1½   cups vegetable stock or water (³/₄ cup when using vegetable burgers)
- 1   16-ounce can tomatoes, chopped, liquid reserved
- 1   16-ounce can red kidney beans, do not drain
- 2   Mexican green chilis in brine, drained, chopped (optional)
      Salt and freshly ground pepper, to taste

Heat oil in large saucepan. Add onion, sauté until golden brown. Add chili powder and TVP, sauté 5 minutes. Add vegetable stock, tomatoes, kidney beans, green chilis and reserved liquid from tomatoes. Cover, simmer 20 minutes.

* TVP can be purchased at specialty health food stores.

6 Servings

Tim McGraw

McGraw's Cajun Gumbo

1	pound smoked hot sausage, sliced
1	pound chicken breasts, cut into cubes
4	tablespoons flour
3	cups okra (frozen is O.K.)
3	onions, chopped
1	bell pepper, chopped
3	stalks celery, chopped
3	garlic cloves, minced
1	15-ounce can tomato sauce
1	cup water
2	teaspoons Tabasco® pepper sauce

Heat heavy large skillet. Add sausage. Cook until browned. Remove from skillet. Add chicken to skillet, brown on all sides. Remove chicken from skillet, set aside with sausage. Sprinkle flour into meat drippings and stir well to form a roux. Cook 2 minutes, stirring continuously. Add okra, onions, bell pepper, celery and garlic. Cook until onions become soft. Return sausage and chicken to skillet. Add tomato sauce and water. Stir over medium heat until thick sauce begins to form. Simmer 1 hour, adding water if necessary. Add Tabasco sauce before serving. Serve over rice. Enjoy!!

8 to 10 Servings

Peanut Butter Kiss Cookies

1	cup smooth peanut butter	3 1/2	cups all-purpose flour
1	cup shortening	2	teaspoons baking soda
1	cup granulated sugar	1	teaspoon salt
1	cup brown sugar	1	cup granulated sugar
2	eggs	1	tablespoon cinnamon
4	tablespoons milk	72	Chocolate Kisses®, unwrapped
2	teaspoons vanilla		

Preheat oven to 375°F. Lightly grease 2 large cookie sheets.

Using electric mixer, beat together peanut butter, shortening and sugars. Add eggs 1 at a time, beating well after each addition. Continue beating until light and fluffy. Beat in vanilla. Sift together flour, baking soda and salt. Add to peanut butter mixture. Shape batter into small round balls. Mix sugar and cinnamon in bowl, roll each cookie in mixture. Place on prepared cookie sheets. Bake 8 minutes. Remove from oven and press chocolate kiss in center of each cookie. Return to oven and bake 2 minutes. Place on waxed paper to cool until kiss is cold and firm.

Makes about 6 Dozen

SARAH MCLACHLAN

In the Kitchen with Sarah McLachlan

Writer's block tends to send me straight to the kitchen. Rumor has it that the aroma of fresh baking stimulates the creative process.

Writer's Block Loaf (Chocolate Chip Banana Bread)

3/4	cup brown sugar
1/2	cup (1 stick) butter, softened
2	eggs
1/2	cup sour cream
1	cup mashed ripe banana
2	cups all-purpose flour
1	teaspoon baking soda
1/2	teaspoon salt
3/4	cup miniature semisweet chocolate chips

Sarah has a "thing" for chocolate.

Preheat oven to 350°F. Lightly grease one 9-inch or two 8-inch loaf pans.

Using electric mixer, blend together sugar and butter. Add eggs 1 at a time, beating well after each addition. Add sour cream, mix well. Add banana, blend well. Sift in dry ingredients, mix well. Fold in chocolate chips; be careful not to over mix.

Pour into pan(s) and bake 40 to 45 minutes or until a toothpick inserted into center comes out clean.

Let cool 15 minutes before removing from pan, then allow to cool completely before slicing or wrapping.

(This loaf is best when stored in the refrigerator.)

6 Servings

Meat Loaf

Cheese Grits Loaf

This dish is very easy to prepare. It may not be on everyone's diet menu, but sometimes you need food for the soul. My whole family enjoys having this as a compliment to our Thanksgiving dinner. Everyone who has tried Cheese Grits Loaf has really liked it and has asked us for the recipe.

4	cups cooked grits
2	eggs, beaten
3	tablespoons Tabasco® pepper sauce
1	tablespoon butter, melted
1	cup cheddar cheese, grated
3	pickled jalapeño peppers, sliced
1	teaspoon freshly ground black pepper

Preheat oven to 350°F.

Stir together grits and eggs. Add Tabasco sauce and butter. Stir in remaining ingredients. Pour into non-stick loaf pan. Bake 25 minutes. Cool for 5 minutes. Invert onto plate. Slice into 1-inch thick pieces for serving.

Served warm with fresh sliced tomato, a green salad, and an enormous pitcher of iced tea, this makes a perfect lunch.

4 servings

Liza Minnelli

Liza's Gazpacho

Ever since I was very young, during the hot summer this has been one of my favorite recipes in the world!

5	cucumbers, peeled and seeds removed
2	green bell peppers, seeded and chopped
1	medium onion, chopped
2-4	cloves garlic, minced
1	8-ounce can peeled tomatoes, chopped
2	slices white bread, torn into pieces
2	10-ounce cans tomato juice
2	egg yolks
	Juice of 1 lemon
3/4	cup olive oil
	Tabasco® pepper sauce, to taste
	Salt and pepper, to taste

In blender or food processor, puree cucumbers, bell peppers, garlic, onion and tomatoes, in batches if necessary. Remove and place in large bowl. Place bread, tomato juice, eggs and lemon juice in blender or food processor. Process until mixture is pureed. Gradually add olive oil until completely emulsified. Add to bowl with vegetable puree, stir to mix completely. Season with Tabasco® sauce, salt and pepper.

5 Servings

68

Moby

Seitan

Seitan? What's seitan? Isn't he the Antichrist? Actually, seitan (pronounced say-tan) is a wheat by-product like bran or wheat germ that is quite similar to meat in appearance and texture. For this recipe you can either make your own seitan from scratch (which, like me, you probably won't) or you can go to your friendly neighborhood health food store and buy a mix or some that is premade.

For this meal you'll need (all organically grown, if possible):

1	cup brown basmati rice, cooked (or regular long-grain brown rice)
2 1/4	cups water
4	good-size sweet potatoes
1	tablespoon olive oil
	Cinnamon
	Sea salt
1	tablespoon vegetable oil
1/2	pound of seitan, cut into cubes*
2	green, yellow, orange, or red bell peppers, cut into strips
	Some fresh ginger, minced
	Some garlic cloves, minced
1	tablespoon tamari or good soy sauce
1	head of broccoli, cut into florets and steamed

Here's what you do:
Place rice and water in a good pot with a tight-fitting lid. Bring to boil, reduce heat to simmer. Cook 35 minutes, turn off heat and let sit covered. While rice is cooking, boil sweet potatoes in large saucepan of water, until tender. Place sweet potatoes and a little bit of liquid in a large bowl. Add olive oil, cinnamon and pinch of sea salt. Using electric mixer, mash until fluffy. Cover and set aside. Heat vegetable oil in a good heavy skillet. Add seitan, bell peppers, ginger and garlic. Sauté 3 to 5 minutes. Add tamari, cook until absorbed. Serve seitan on rice with mashed sweet potatoes and steamed broccoli. This is a wonderful dish, inexpensive, easy to make, low in fat, high in fiber, protein and vitamins—good for you and good for the earth. Total kitchen time is around an hour.

* Substitute tempeh or tofu for the seitan if you're allergic to wheat or if you don't like or can't find seitan. For condiments you can sprinkle tamari, black pepper, toasted sesame seeds, sea salt, or sea shake, or whatever suits your fancy.

4 Servings

RANDY NEWMAN

Randy Newman's Primitive Cheese Sandwich

3   slices Old English® cheddar cheese
2   slices white bread

Place cheese between bread slices, stacking carefully. I like to accompany the sandwich with a simple muscatel or, for a more formal luncheon, with a brisk shot or two of rye.

I Serving   *Randy Newman*

EDDIE MONEY

Eddie's Quick and Easy Rock and Roll Chicken

Chicken
2   frying chickens, whole, insides removed
2   tablespoons butter, melted
1/4   teaspoon rosemary
      Salt and pepper, to taste

Preheat oven to 350°F.

Stuffing
1   tablespoon olive oil
6   slices white bread, torn into pieces
1 1/2   cups milk
1   egg, lightly beaten
      Salt and pepper, to taste
1/4   cup finely chopped onion
1/4   cup chopped celery
4   pork sausages, crumbled, cooked

For chicken:
Rinse and dry chickens. Baste with butter and rub inside and out with rosemary, salt and pepper.

For stuffing:
Heat oil in large skillet. Mix together bread, milk, egg, salt and pepper. Mix until bread completely absorbs moisture. Set aside. Place onion, celery and sausage in skillet, cook until golden brown. Add bread mixture. Cook 2 minutes. Remove from heat.

Using large spoon, place stuffing mixture in cavity of chicken. Do not overstuff. Bake 1 1/2 hours or until outside is golden brown, basting frequently.

Note: With the chicken, I serve mashed potatoes, buttered brussels sprouts, cranberry sauce, gravy, cornbread and apple cider.

8 Servings

Neville Brothers

Our whole family loves to cook! We have all been brought up with the New Orleans style of cooking, spicing up the taste of all our food!

Aaron's Oyster Stuffing

1 loaf French bread (stale is best)
1/2 cup (1 stick) butter
1 onion, chopped
1/2 bell pepper, chopped
4 garlic cloves, minced
4 scallions, chopped
1 celery stalk, chopped
2 dozen oysters, juice reserved
1 parsley sprig
Salt and pepper, to taste

Chop bread in food processor to make bread crumbs. Melt butter in large skillet. Add onion, bell pepper, garlic, scallions, celery and parsley, cook 15 minutes or until tender.

Add oysters. Cut oysters in half using spoon. Sauté 2 minutes. Add bread crumbs, mix well, continue to cook over low heat. Pour oyster juice evenly over skillet ingredients. Season with salt and pepper. Add water, if too dry.

6 to 8 Servings

Brother's Fried Eggplant Strips

2 eggs, beaten
1/2 cup milk
2 teaspoons Tabasco® pepper sauce
1/2 teaspoon cayenne pepper
1/2 teaspoon black pepper
1 eggplant, cut into 3-inch strips
1/2 cup flour
Bread crumbs, the spicy seasoned type are best
Vegetable oil for frying

Mix eggs, milk, Tabasco® sauce, cayenne and black peppers. Dust eggplant lightly with flour on all sides. Dip into egg mixture. Cover completely with bread crumbs. Heat large skillet filled 1/2 full with oil. Fry breaded eggplant slowly until golden brown.

4 Servings

Willie Nelson

Willie's All-Time Favorite Salmon Cakes

2   eggs, beaten
1   tablespoon lemon juice
1   teaspoon Dijon mustard
1   cup fresh bread crumbs
1   stalk celery,
      finely chopped
1   tablespoon grated onion
1   teaspoon dill
1/2 teaspoon salt
      Dash cayenne pepper
1   15-ounce can red salmon,
      flaked, boneless, skinless,
      liquid reserved
1   cup chopped pecans
      or almonds
      Vegetable oil
      Lemon wedges
1   tablespoon fresh parsley,
      chopped

Mix together eggs, lemon juice and mustard. Add bread crumbs, celery, onion, dill, salt and cayenne pepper. Mix well. Add salmon with reserved juice. Form into small patties. Press nuts into sides of patties. Heat oil in heavy-bottom skillet. Cook patties on both sides until lightly browned. Serve with lemon wedges and parsley.

4-6 Servings

JESSYE NORMAN

Jessye Norman's Quick Dessert Cake

3	eggs
3/4	cup (1 1/2 sticks) unsalted butter
3/4	cup brown sugar
1 1/2	teaspoons lemon essence
1/4	cup Grand Marnier® liqueur
1/4	cup milk
1 3/4	cups self-rising flour
3	teaspoons baking powder
3/4	teaspoon salt
1/4	cup chopped almonds
1/4	cup raisins

Preheat oven to 350F. Lightly grease and flour 13x9x2-inch cake pan.

Using electric mixer, beat together eggs, butter, brown sugar, lemon essence, Grand Marnier® and milk. Mix on medium speed 4 minutes. Sift together flour, baking powder and salt, add to egg mixture. Add almonds and raisins, mix well. Let sit 10 minutes. Mix on high speed 2 minutes. Pour into prepared pan. Bake 45 minutes or until toothpick inserted into center comes out clean.

This cake makes a fine accompaniment for fresh fruit salad or ice cream.

6 to 8 Servings

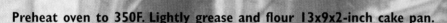

K.T. Oslin

K.T. Oslin's 40-Clove Garlic Chicken

1	2 1/2-pound roasting chicken, whole, insides removed
2	tablespoons olive oil
1	teaspoon each: fresh sage, basil and thyme, chopped
	Salt and pepper, to taste
3	heads garlic, cloves separated, peeled

Preheat oven to 350°F.

Mix together oil, herbs, salt and pepper, to form paste. Rub herb mixture over chicken. Fill chicken cavity with garlic. Place chicken in large Dutch oven. Cover and bake 1 hour. Serve with lots

LORRIE MORGAN

Lorrie's Simply-Good Orange Cake

Cake
2	cups sugar
2	eggs
1	16-ounce can mandarin oranges
2	cups all-purpose flour
2	teaspoons baking soda
1/2	teaspoon salt

Glaze
3/4	cup brown sugar

Preheat oven to 350°F.

For cake:
Grease and flour 13x9x2-inch cake pan. Using electric mixer, beat together sugar and eggs. Stir in oranges. Sift flour, baking soda and salt into mixture. Mix well. Pour into prepared cake pan. Bake 35 minutes, or until toothpick inserted into center comes out clean.

For glaze:
Place ingredients in small saucepan. Bring to boil over medium heat. Cook until mixture becomes thick and syrupy. Pour over cake as it leaves oven. Let cake cool. Serve with fresh whipped cream.

6 Servings

DOLLY PARTON

I love this dessert almost as much as
I love singing this song!

Islands in the Stream

3   eggs, separated
2/3   cup sugar
2   tablespoons flour
4   cups milk
1   teaspoon vanilla
     Boiling water
     Nutmeg, optional

Using electric mixer, beat together egg
yolks and sugar, until smooth. Add flour
and mix well. Heat milk in saucepan, until
skin forms on top. Do not boil. Add a
little bit of milk to egg mixture to warm
eggs. Add egg mixture to milk. Cook on
low heat, stirring constantly. Cook 20 to
25 minutes, until mixture becomes thick.
Remove from heat; add vanilla.

Using electric mixer or whisk, whip egg whites. Add boiling water 1 teaspoon at a time,
until egg whites harden. Using spatula, place egg-white mixture on top of milk mixture.
Sprinkle with nutmeg. Chill before serving.

4 Servings

Peter, Paul & Mary

Mary's Pea Soup

I like this as a main course—with good French bread and a salad.

I	pound dried split peas, rinsed
10	cups of water
2	cups of chicken stock
4	large onions, chopped
I	large bunch celery, chopped
	Good sized butt end of smoked ham with bone, remove meat from bone, cut into large pieces, discard fat
I	tablespoon Tabasco® pepper sauce
I	bay leaf
¹/₂	cup heavy cream (optional)
	Salt and pepper, to taste

Place peas in heavy large Dutch oven. Add water, broth, vegetables, and bone. Add meat and Tabasco, bring to boil. Reduce heat, add bay leaf, let simmer until peas become soft, about I hour.

With large spoon, remove meat and bay leaf from pot, reserve meat, discard bay leaf. Puree the pea soup in blender. Pour pea soup back into Dutch oven, add meat and stir in cream, if desired. Season with salt and pepper.

8 Servings

Jalapeno Maize – Paul's Recipe for Corn Muffins

2¹/₂	cups whole wheat flour
I	cup corn meal
¹/₂	cup rice flour
I¹/₂	tablespoon baking powder
¹/₂	teaspoon sea salt
¹/₂	cup corn oil
¹/₄	cup maple syrup
¹/₂	cup plain soy milk
2	cups apple juice
¹/₂	tablespoon vanilla
¹/₄	cup Jalapenos

Preheat oven to 350° F. Lightly grease 12 muffin-pan cups.

Mix together dry ingredients. Beat together oil, syrup, soy milk, apple juice, and vanilla. Add dry ingredients, mix well. Add Jalapenos. Pour batter evenly into muffin-pan cups. Bake 20-25 minutes or until a toothpick inserted in the center comes out clean.

12 Servings

Puff's Favorite Salad
By Peter Yarrow

Salad

1 6-ounce can tuna fish packed in water

2 tomatoes, cut into eight sections

1 cucumber, peeled and sliced

1 head Boston or romaine lettuce, washed and torn into bite-size pieces

8 radishes, halved

2 heads Belgian endive, leaves separated

Dressing

1 large garlic clove, crushed

3/4 cup virgin olive oil

1/4 cup balsamic vinegar

2 tablespoons Dijon mustard

1 teaspoon Worcestershire sauce

1 teaspoon fresh lemon juice

4 drops Tabasco® pepper sauce

1/4 cup finely grated Romano or Parmesan cheese

Salad:

Toss together all ingredients. Pour desired amount of dressing over salad and toss to cover evenly. Sprinkle with cheese. Serve.

Dressing:

Marinate crushed garlic cloves in olive oil 30 minutes. Remove garlic from oil and discard. Mix together balsamic vinegar, mustard, Worcestershire sauce, lemon juice and Tabasco sauce. Add oil gradually, whisking ingredients to incorporate thoroughly.

6 to 8 Servings

Shabba Ranks

Steamed Fish

1/2	cup (1 stick) butter
2	small onions, finely sliced
2	small tomatoes, chopped
6	okra, sliced
1	jalapeño pepper, diced
1/2	cup water
1	tablespoon ketchup
1/2	teaspoon salt
	Pinch black pepper
2	pounds red snapper, cleaned, scales remove

Melt butter in heavy large skillet. Add onion, sauté 3 minutes. Add tomatoes, jalapeño, okra, water, ketchup, salt and pepper. Bring to boil. Add fish, reduce heat. Simmer until fish is tender, about 20 minutes. Serve over rice or with crackers.

4 Servings

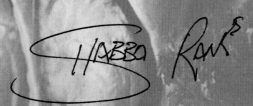

Lou Reed
Laurie Anderson

Hot Pastrami Sandwich

Order hot pastrami sandwich with mustard on rye from Carnegie Deli, NYC. Eat with pickles.

2 Servings

Dianne Reeves

Dianne's Monkey Bread

2/3	cup sugar
2	packages active dry yeast
8	cups all-purpose flour
1	cup warm water, 105° to 115°F
1	cup shortening
2	cups milk
4	eggs
1	teaspoon salt
	Melted butter

Mix together sugar, yeast, 2 cups flour. Add water, mix well. Set aside.

Melt shortening in saucepan. Add milk. Using electric mixer or whisk, beat eggs in large bowl. Gradually add melted shortening and milk to eggs. Add sugar mixture. Stir in remaining flour and salt. Mix well, until dough forms ball, free from the sides of the bowl.

Cover dough with a clean cloth. Let rise 1 hour in warm place.

Divide dough into 2 portions. Knead each half until smooth. Using floured rolling pin, roll dough out into 1/2-inch thickness. Cut into circles with 2-inch-diameter cookie cutter.

Dip each roll in melted butter, line up in 10-inch tube pan. Continue until all rolls are layered into pan. Let rise until doubled.

Preheat oven to 375°F. Brush bread with melted butter. Bake 45 minutes.

8 Servings

Peanut butter 'N jelly pancakes

Make 4 servings

10 **CHIPS AHOY!** Chocolate Chip
   Cookies, finely rolled (about
   1 cup crumbs)
1½ cups buttermilk baking mix
2 eggs
1 cup milk
½ cup creamy peanut butter
¼ cup jam or preserves, any flavor
Confectioners' sugar
Pancake syrup

In bowl, beat together cookie
crumbs, baking mix, eggs
and milk until smooth.

On lightly greased
preheated griddle
or skillet, pour
⅔ cup batter,
spreading to
7-inch circle.
Cook over
medium heat until
surface is bubbly and
bottom is lightly browned. Turn carefully to
brown other side. Remove and keep warm.
Repeat to make a total of 4 pancakes. Spread
2 pancakes with peanut butter and 1 with jam.
Alternately stack pancakes beginning with peanut
butter-topped pancake and ending with plain pancake. Sprinkle with
confectioners' sugar.

Cut pancake stack into wedges; serve immediately with syrup.
Wedges may be wrapped and stored in freezer.

MICROWAVE REHEAT DIRECTIONS: Unwrap one frozen wedge
(¼ stack); place on microwave-safe plate. Microwave, uncovered, at
HIGH (100% power) about 1½ minutes or until hot.

RESTLESS HEART

Restless Heart's Oklahoma Pull-Aparts

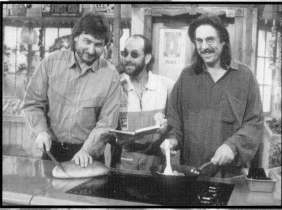

1	package active dry yeast
1/2	cup sugar
1	cup milk, scalded and cooled to 105° to 115°F
3/4	cup (1 1/2 sticks) butter, melted
1 1/2	teaspoons salt
3	eggs, beaten
4	cups all-purpose flour

Melted butter

Mix together yeast, sugar and milk. Add butter, salt and eggs. Gradually add flour. Mix well. Cover with clean cloth and let sit 2 hours.

Divide dough into 3 portions. Form each portion into 1/2-inch-thick squares, 6-inches wide, on floured surface. Lightly grease three 8-inch round cake pans. Cut into 1/2-inch strips. Dip each strip in melted butter. Wind first strip into coil, place on prepared cake pan. Wrap next strip around coil, lining up ends. Continue until coil meets edges of pan. Repeat with remaining dough.

Let rise 1 1/2 hours in warm place. Preheat oven to 350°F. Bake 25 minutes.

12 Servings

COWBOY JUNKIES

Margo Timmins' Cowboy Junkie Chicken for Chicken Junkie Cowboys

2	tablespoons olive oil
2	tablespoons soy sauce
2	tablespoons Dijon mustard
2	tablespoons rice vinegar
4	boneless chicken breasts

Mix together olive oil, soy sauce, mustard and vinegar. Place chicken breasts in olive oil mixture and let sit 1 hour. Broil or grill chicken 7 to 10 minutes, each side.

Mmm! Goody!!

4 Servings

THE ROLLING STONES

Mick Jagger's Shrimp Curry

This recipe is one of my favorites from an old friend fromIndia.

1/4	cup ghee (clarified butter)
1	medium onion, diced
	Curry powder
	Bay leaf (leaves)
1	12-ounce can coconut cream
1	cup boiling water
1/2	teaspoon Garam Masala
1	generous handful fresh coriander
	Juice of 1/2 lime
1	pound small prawns, washed, peeled, deveined

Garam Masala:

2	teaspoons coriander
4	teaspoons cumin
1	teaspoon cloves
2	teaspoons black pepper
1	teaspoon cinnamon
1	teaspoon nutmeg

For shrimp curry:
Heat the ghee in a heavy large saucepan. Add onion and sauté until onion is translucent.
Add curry powder to suit your taste (approximately 1 to 2 teaspoons). Add bay leaf or
two. At this point you should add the coconut cream and boiling water. Add Garam
Masala, coriander and lime juice. At this stage add the shrimp, bring to boil.
Serve immediately.

As accompanying side dishes, a good combination is basmati rice and an assortment of
the following condiments: Dall (lentils), cucumber, tomatoes, chutney, raisins, peanuts and
Aerosmith's Vegetable Vindaloo.

For Garam Masala:
This delicate combination of spices is made by mixing together all ingredients. Store
remainder in airtight container.
4 Servings

Beggars Banquet by Ronnie Wood, oil on canvas: 1988

Keith Richard's Shepherds Pie

The one food I can eat 365 days a year is Shepherds Pie. On tour, at home, wherever; I guess growing up back home in England my mother never thought her recipe would be my favorite daily meal to this day!

3	pounds potatoes, peeled, diced
1	tablespoon butter
	Salt and pepper, to taste
2	pounds ground beef
2	large onions, chopped
2	large carrots, grated
1	12-ounce can beef stock
1	tablespoon corn starch

Place potatoes in large saucepan, cover with water. Bring to boil, reduce heat, simmer until tender. Drain. Using electric mixer or whisk, mash potatoes and butter. Season with salt and pepper. Set aside.

Heat large skillet. Add beef and onions. Season with salt and pepper. Add carrots and stock. Mix in corn starch, cook ten minutes. Pour into pie dish and top with mashed potatoes. Place under broiler until potatoes begin to turn brown.

6 Servings

Lee Ritenour

Broiled Chilean Sea Bass with Roasted Potatoes

Fish

2	Fillets of Chilean sea bass (fresh, not frozen)
	Olive oil
	Juice of 1 lemon
	Salt and pepper, to taste
2	shallots, minced
	Fresh parsley, minced

Potatoes

3	medium baking potatoes, peeled, diced
4	garlic cloves, minced
	Salt and pepper, to taste

For fish:
Rinse fillets and pat dry. Coat lightly with olive oil, 1 teaspoon lemon juice, salt and pepper. Refrigerate 1 hour. Place under broiler, cook 8 minutes. Turn, cover with remaining lemon juice, shallots and parsley. Cook until it flakes easily with Fork, (about 8 to 10 more minutes).

For potatoes:
Preheat oven to 375°F. Place potatoes in medium saucepan, cover with water. Bring to boil. Reduce heat, let simmer 10 minutes, until easily pierced with fork. Do not overcook. Drain, toss with garlic, salt and pepper. Spread onto baking sheet and bake until golden brown.

3 tp 4 Servings

RuPaul

Breakfast Cush Cush

This is the equivalent of pan-fried corn bread but it's served like hot cereal. To this day, my sisters and I make it when we're together. It's the ultimate in comfort food.

6	cups water
1/2	teaspoon salt
1 1/2	cups yellow cornmeal
1	teaspoon Crisco® shortening
1	cup milk, heated
2	tablespoons sugar
1	tablespoon butter

Bring water and salt to boil in medium saucepan. Reduce heat and stir in cornmeal. Cook over low heat, stirring constantly, until thick, about 15 minutes.

Melt shortening in large nonstick, skillet, spoon cornmeal mixture into skillet. Cook until lightly browned, stir, cook 2 to 3 minutes.

Place "Cush Cush" into serving bowls, top with heated milk, sugar and butter; mix well and eat.

2 Servings

Salt 'n Pepa

Jerk Chicken

Our favorite recipe!

6-8	medium onions, chopped		2	teaspoons pimento berries
1	scallion, chopped		1	teaspoon celery seeds
2	cloves garlic, minced		1/2	teaspoon oregano
1	cup soy sauce		1/2	teaspoon thyme
1/4	cup oil		1/2	teaspoon rosemary
3	scotch bonnet or jalapeño peppers, minced (careful, they're hot!)		1/2	teaspoon tarragon
1	2 1/2 lb. chicken			Salt 'n Pepa to taste

Combine all ingredients, except chicken. Place chicken in large baking dish and cover with marinade. Let sit at least 6 to 10 hours (overnight is best).

To cook:
Preheat oven to 375° F. Remove chicken from marinade and place on broiler pan or cookie sheet. Bake 30 minutes, basting with marinade twice. Remove from oven and place on grill or under broiler 20-30 minutes. Salt 'n Pepa to taste!

4 to 6 Servings

David Sanborn

David's Killer Coconut, Pineapple, Walnut Carrot Cake

Everything goes better with music, we recommend James Brown or Django Reinhardt. Also a couple of lit candles in the kitchen makes cooking and baking much cozier. Have fun!

Cake

1¹/₂ cups all-purpose flour	3 eggs
¹/₂ cup whole-wheat flour	1 cup light-brown sugar
2¹/₂ teaspoons baking soda	1 8-ounce can crushed
2 teaspmon	pineapple
1 teaspoon salt	1¹/₂ cups coconut flakes
1 cup sugar	2 cups grated carrots
1 cup vegetable oil	1 cup chopped walnuts

Frosting

1 16-ounce pkg. cream cheese, softened
¹/₄ cup (¹/₂ stick) butter
3 cups confectioners' sugar
1 tablespoon milk
¹/₂ teaspoon vanilla
1¹/₂ cups coconut flakes

For cake:

Preheat oven to 350° F. Lightly grease two 10-inch pans. Line bottom of pans with wax or parchment paper.

Sift together dry ingredients. Set aside. With electric mixer, beat together sugar and oil. Add eggs one at a time until mixed thoroughly. Mix in brown sugar. Add dry ingredients and mix until smooth. Stir in pineapple, coconut, carrots, and nuts; mix well. Batter should be very wet and gooey. Pour into prepared pans. Bake for approximately 50 minutes or until a toothpick inserted into center comes out clean. The cake should be moist and golden brown. Let cool 15 minutes before removing cakes from pans.

For frosting: Blend together cream cheese and butter. Add sugar, milk and vanilla; mix well. Add 3/4 cup coconut. Place remaining coconut on baking sheet and toast under broiler, watching closely; set aside. Place 1 cake layer on plate; spread frosting evenly over top. Repeat with remaining layers. Spread remaining frosting evenly over sides of cake. Cover cake with the toasted coconut. Voila. 6 to 8 servings

The Sanborn's Healthy Roasted Free Range Chicken

1 large free range chicken (3 1/2 to 4 lbs)
1 large spanish onion, chopped
1 red onion, chopped
4 cups sliced mushrooms(shitake, crimini, portobello)
1 leek, sliced
1 small turnip or daikon, chopped
3 cloves of garlic, minced
2 lemons, one of them sliced in 1/4 inch slices on the short angle.
   fresh rosemary and thyme
   herb salt and pepper to taste

Clean chicken, rub it with rosemary and place it breastside up in roasting pan with the vegetables around it. Squeeze the juice from one of the lemons over it. Make a two inch incision in the skin across the thickest point of each breast with a sharp knife, and slide a slice of lemon (yes, with the peel on) under the skin between the meat and the skin. Make a couple of small incisions more on each breast towards the back and place garlic slices under them. Stick rosemary and thyme under the skin with the lemon and between the wings and the body. Season with herb salt, pepper, and whatever other spices you like on chicken that won't overpower the taste of the lemon and the rosemary. Pour two cups of water in the bottom of the pan so it won't dry while roasting. Place in preheated oven at 400 degrees for approximately one hour and 30 minutes. Baste it a few times if you have the time. If not, no sweat.
This chicken is great with pureed sweet potatoes and the vegetables the chicken was cooked with, or mashed potatoes.

Seal

Penne á la Seal's
Special Sauce

6	tablespoons olive oil
1 1/2	cups water
1	medium onion, chopped
5	garlic cloves, minced
1	28-ounce can crushed plum tomatoes
1	cup sun-dried tomatoes, soaked in warm water 15 minutes, drained, chopped
1/2	cup white wine
1	pound penne pasta, cooked
1	head broccoli, cut into florets, steamed
	oregano, basil, salt and pepper to taste

Heat 4 tablespoons of oil in heavy large saucepan. Add onion, sauté until translucent. Add crushed tomatoes and water. Add oregano, basil, salt and pepper to taste. Cook 45 minutes; simmer 15 minutes.

In large skillet heat 2 tablespoons oil. Add garlic. Sauté 3 minutes. Add sun-dried tomatoes, sauté 3 minutes. Add wine. Cook 5 minutes. Pour into tomato mixture. Cook 15 minutes. Serve over pasta with broccoli.

This is a wonderful dish.

4 Servings

Frank Sinatra

Blue Eyes' Italian Chicken, Potato and Onion dish

This is best with soft music and candlelight.

2	2-pound chickens, cut into pieces
	Olive oil
2	medium onions, sliced, separated
8	potatoes, peeled, quartered
1	cup white wine
2	tablespoons oregano
1	cup fresh parsley, minced
	Salt and pepper, to taste
1	lemon, sliced

Preheat oven to 350°F.

Soak chicken in salted water 30 minutes. Drain. Pat dry with paper towels. Fill large baking dish 1/2 to 3/4 inch high with olive oil. Layer chicken in bottom of pan in 1 layer. Cover with onions. Cover with potatoes, wine, oregano, parsley, salt and pepper. Mix pan ingredients by hand. Cover with lemon slices. Cover with foil. Bake 1 hour and 15 minutes, stirring every 20 minutes. Uncover and cook 15 minutes, or until potatoes are soft.

Serve with cold white wine...and you'll love it. Add a salad and a dessert, and it is a wonderful meal.

8 Servings

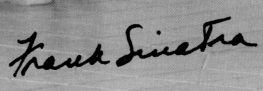

Sonic Youth

Chocolate Mousse
(Experimental Moose Trash)

8	ounces bittersweet chocolate
4	eggs, separated
	Zest of 1 orange

Melt chocolate in heavy saucepan on very low heat. Add egg yolks
1 at a time, beating well after each addition. Add 1/2 orange zest.
In separate bowl, beat egg whites into stiff peaks. Fold small
amount of egg whites into chocolate mixture. Gently fold chocolate
mixture into remaining egg whites.

Pour into individual serving dishes and chill several hours.

Sprinkle with remaining orange zest. Serve.   4 Servings

WILD COLONIALS

Wild Colonial Risotto
The Truth and Nothing but the Truth

1	ounce dried porcini mushrooms
3/4	cup (1 1/2 sticks) butter
1	onion, diced
2	cups Arborio rice
4	14 1/2-ounce cans chicken stock
1/2	cup fresh-grated Parmesan cheese

Soak porcini mushrooms 1 hour. Drain and squeeze to
eliminate remaining moisture.

Melt butter in heavy large saucepan. Add onion, cook until
soft. Add rice, stir. Add mushrooms and 1 can stock. When
liquid has been absorbed add another can stock. Continue to
stir and add stock until risotto is al dente, about
30 minutes. Remove from heat. Add Parmesan cheese. Cover
and let sit. Sit down a minute and rest. Then serve.

4 Servings

SOUL ASYLUM

Karl Mueller's Annual BBQ Rib-off Recipe

2	12-ounce beers
1	large onion, quartered
1/4	cup Tabasco® pepper sauce
1	tablespoon crushed red pepper
20	garlic cloves
3	racks baby back ribs

Place beer, onion, Tabasco sauce, crushed red pepper and garlic in large stock pot. Bring to boil. Add ribs. Let simmer 20 minutes. Remove ribs, rub with "rendezvous" dry BBQ Rib Spice (Call "Rendezvous" in Memphis, TN and they'll Fedex it to you). Let sit 20 minutes.

Place on charcoal grill. Cook 7 to 10 minutes each side.

Serve 'em up.

Note: Serve with an assortment of barbecue sauces. "Rendezvous" also has a great barbecue sauce.

Also, you must wear an Elvis apron with microphone mitten.

Very Important make sure you have lots of extra beer because you will get hot standing by that barbecue.

6 Servings

SPONGE

Joey's Loco Love Salsa

12	medium Roma tomatoes, finely diced
10	medium banana peppers (5 inches long, yellow-green color), minced
3	medium jalapeño peppers, finely diced
1	medium onion, finely diced
2	garlic cloves, minced
1 1/2	tablespoons cilantro, chopped
	Juice of 1 1/2 large lemons
1 1/2	tablespoons olive oil
	Large dose of Tabasco® pepper sauce
	Salt and pepper, to taste

Combine tomatoes, banana peppers, jalapeño peppers, onion, garlic and cilantro in large bowl. Mix well. Stir in lemon juice, olive oil and Tabasco sauce. Season with salt and pepper. Chill 30 minutes. Serve with your favorite chips.

For low-fat chips, try baking your own by using fresh flower or corn tortillas. Cut into chip-size pieces and bake 15 minutes or until crispy at 325°F.

5 Servings for really hungry people...

Spin Doctors

Spin Doctors Chocolate Cream Pie
Easy and delicious

Buy or make deep dish pie crust
2 boxes of cooked chocolate pudding, not instant
8oz. heavy cream

Bake crust as directed and let cool

Cook pudding, follow directions as appear on box
Put pudding in crust
Let cool and refrigerate for 2 hours

Whip the heavy cream. Add to top of pie

Eat

THE TEMPTATIONS

The Temptations' "DELIGHT"

2	15-ounce cans tomato sauce
1/2	bottle ketchup
1	16-ounce can whole tomatoes
2	medium onions, sliced
	Pinch of sugar
	Dash of garlic powder
	Salt and pepper, to taste

1	whole chicken, cut into pieces, rinsed, dried
	Juice of 1 lemon
	Salt, pepper, garlic powder, onion powder, to taste

2	tablespoons olive oil

Place tomato sauce, ketchup, whole tomatoes, onions, sugar and garlic powder in large stockpot. Bring to boil. Reduce heat and simmer above ingredients in medium to large pot and simmer 10 minutes.

Cover chicken with lemon juice and seasonings. Heat oil in large skillet. Add chicken. Cook until brown on all sides. Transfer chicken to paper towels to absorb excess oil. Place chicken in pot with tomato sauce. Cover with lid, cook 45 minutes over medium heat.

Serve "DELIGHT" over rice.

4 to 6 Servings

OREO CHEESECAKE

Makes 12 servings

1 (20-ounce) package OREO Chocolate Sandwich Cookies
⅓ cup FLEISCHMANN'S Margarine, melted
3 (8-ounce) packages cream cheese, softened
¾ cup sugar
4 eggs, at room temperature
1 cup dairy sour cream
1 teaspoon vanilla extract
Whipped cream, for garnish

Finely roll 30 cookies; coarsely chop 20 cookies. In bowl, combine finely rolled cookie crumbs and margarine. Press on bottom and 2 inches up side of 9-inch springform pan; set aside.

In bowl, with electric mixer at medium speed, beat cream cheese and sugar until creamy. Blend in eggs, sour cream and vanilla; fold in chopped cookies. Spread mixture into prepared crust. Bake at 350° for 60 minutes or until set.

Cool on wire rack at room temperature. Chill at least 4 hours. Halve remaining cookies; remove side of pan. To serve, garnish with whipped cream and cookie halves.

LIVE
Chad's Broccoli Casserole

2	Packages frozen chopped broccoli (cooked)
1	can cream of mushroom soup
1/2	cup mayonaise
2	herbal stuffing
1/4	cup grated onion
1	tablespoon lemon juice
2	cups grated cheese (your preference, I like chedder)
1	beaten egg
	Salt and pepper

Cook broccoli and drain. Combine other ingredients. Add broccoli and pour into a greased 2 quart casserole dish. Bake 350⁰ for about 45 minutes. Before putting into oven you may sprinkle cheese on top.

THEY MIGHT BE GIANTS

This is pretty much my mother's recipe for French toast. It's foolproof and power-packed with calories. No substitutions, please. This is my only recipe and it is responsible for 20% of my current body weight.

John Flansburgh's French Toast

4	slices whole-wheat bread
2	eggs
1	tablespoon milk
2	tablespoons (1/4 stick) butter
	Cinnamon

Beat together eggs and milk in medium bowl. Dunk bread in egg and milk mixture, leave until bread absorbs a good amount of egg and milk. Melt butter in a large skillet. Place soaked bread in skillet and freely sprinkle top of bread with cinnamon. Cook until golden brown on both sides. Serve with real 100% Vermont maple syrup.

4 Servings

Randy Travis

Oatmeal Cookies

1	cup raisins	1	teaspoon baking soda
1	cup water	1	teaspoon salt
3/4	cup shortening	1	teaspoon cinnamon
1 1/2	cups sugar	1/2	teaspoon baking powder
2	eggs	1/2	teaspoon cloves
1	teaspoon vanilla	2	cups oats
2 1/2	cups all-purpose flour	1/2	cup chopped nuts

Preheat oven to 400°F.

Place raisins and water in small saucepan. Bring to boil. Let simmer until raisins are plump, about 15 minutes. Drain, reserving liquid. Add water to reserved liquid to yield 1/2 cup.

Using electric mixer, beat together shortening, sugar, eggs and vanilla. Add reserved liquid. Sift in flour, baking soda, salt, cinnamon, baking powder and cloves. Stir in oats and chopped nuts. Drop dough by rounded teaspoonfuls about 2 inches apart onto ungreased baking sheet. Bake 8 to 10 minutes, until light brown.

Makes about 6 Dozen

Randy Travis

Pam Tillis

Pam's Vegetable Pie

1	10-inch prepared pie shell
3	tablespoons butter
1	pound fresh mushrooms, sliced
1	medium onion, sliced
2	zucchini or yellow squash, sliced
1	green bell pepper, sliced
1	teaspoon salt
1/4	teaspoon black pepper
	Dash of garlic salt
1	tomato, sliced
1	cup mayonnaise
1	cup mozzarella cheese, grated

Preheat oven to 325°F. Bake pie shell 20 minutes.

Melt butter in large skillet. Add vegetables and sauté 5 to 10 minutes; drain and season with salt, pepper and garlic salt. Line bottom of pie shell with tomato slices, cover with vegetable mixture. Combine mayonnaise and cheese in small bowl, spread over vegetables and bake uncovered 45 minutes to 1 hour.

6 Servings

Pam Tillis

Tony Toni Tone

Timothy Christian Riley's Sweet Potato-Pie

4	large sweet potatoes
1/2	cup (1 stick) butter
2	cups sugar
4	eggs
1	teaspoon cinnamon
1/2	teaspoon salt
1/2	teaspoon nutmeg
1	tablespoon vanilla
1	20-ounce can evaporated milk
1	teaspoon lemon juice
1	prepared pie crust, uncooked

Preheat oven to 350°F.

Place sweet potatoes in large pot. Cover with water. Bring to boil, cook until easily pierced with a fork. Let cool. Peel.

Using electric mixer, beat sweet potatoes with butter and sugar. Add eggs 1 at a time, beating well after each addition. Add cinnamon, salt, nutmeg, vanilla and milk. Mix well. Pour into pie crust. Bake 1 hour and 15 minutes, or until toothpick inserted into center comes out clean.

"Just like Mama used to make."

8 Servings

Timothy Riley

Tony, Toni, Tone'

Travis Tritt

Travis Tritt's Hot and Spicy Chili

1	pound ground beef
2	15-ounce cans kidney beans, drained
2	14 1/2-ounce cans stewed tomatoes
1	6-ounce can tomato paste
1	12-ounce can beer
1	large bell pepper, chopped coarsely
1	medium white onion, chopped coarsely
2	tablespoons chili powder
1	garlic clove, minced
3	tablespoons mustard
2	tablespoons basil
1/2	teaspoon oregano
2	jalapeño peppers, sliced
	Seasoned salt, to taste
	Shredded cheese
	Tabasco® pepper sauce to taste

Heat large skillet. Add ground beef. Cook until browned. Drain fat. Transfer to Crock-Pot®. Add remaining ingredients, mix well. Cook on low 8 to 10 hours or on high 3 to 4 hours.
Cover with your favorite shredded cheese and Tabasco sauce. Enjoy.

P.S. Have plenty of Pepto-Bismol on hand.
6 Servings

Marty Stuart

Hilda Stuart's Tea Punch

4	cups boiling water
6	small tea bags
1 1/2	cups sugar
1	12-ounce can frozen lemonade
1	12-ounce can frozen limeade

Steep tea bags in water 10 minutes. Add sugar, lemonade and limeade. Add water to yield 8 cups (1 gallon).

8 Servings

Aunt Jessie Darby's Pineapple Carrot Salad

2	3-ounce packages orange gelatin dessert
2	tablespoons sugar
3	cups hot water
3	tablespoons white vinegar
4	carrots, grated
1	20-ounce can crushed pineapple with syrup

Mix together gelatin and sugar. Stir in water and vinegar; mix until dissolved. Add carrots and pineapple. Pour into serving dish. Chill until set, about 1 hour.

6 Servings

TANYA TUCKER

Tanya's Favorite Cornbread

1 1/2	cups cornmeal
1/3	cup whole-wheat flour
1	teaspoon salt
1	teaspoon baking soda
1	egg, beaten
2	cups buttermilk
2	tablespoons honey

Preheat oven to 350°F.

Mix together dry ingredients. In separate bowl, mix egg, buttermilk and honey. Add to dry ingredients. Stir until mixed, but not smooth. Pour into cast iron skillet. Bake 20 minutes.

Cornbread Dressing

3/4	cup (1 1/2 sticks) butter
1	medium onion, chopped
1 1/4	cups celery, chopped
1/4	cup fresh parsley, chopped
3/4	teaspoon salt
1/2	teaspoon paprika
1/8	teaspoon nutmeg
1 1/4	cups mushrooms, chopped
2	tablespoons white wine
2	large eggs, beaten
1 1/2	cups pecans, chopped
1	recipe Cornbread (as prepared by above directions), crumbled

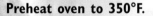

Preheat oven to 350°F. Rub bottom and sides of large baking dish with butter. Melt butter in large skillet. Add onion, cook until soft. Add celery, parsley, salt, paprika, nutmeg, mushrooms and wine. Let simmer 3 minutes. Place cornbread in large bowl. Add skillet ingredients, eggs and pecans. Stir well. Place in prepared baking dish. Bake 30 minutes.

8 Servings

SAMMY HAGAR
Van Halen

CABO WABO TACOS

2	pounds Skirt, Flank or whatever type of steak you prefer. (1/2 to 3/4 thick)
1/2	teaspoon oregano leaves
1/8	cup red wine vinegar
1/8	cup olive oil
	ground pepper

Mix together oregano, vinegar, olive oil and pepper. Place steak in mixture and let sit for at least 1 hour at room temperature turning meat three or four times. On a BBQ Grill, place steak 4 to 5 inches from very hot coals for 5 to 6 minutes per side for medium rare. When done slice into thin strips. Place in warm corn or flour tortillas with salsa and avocado slices.

CABO WABO SALSA:
My <u>personal</u> salsa recipe.

4	small Roma tomatoes (or 2 large regular), diced into small pieces
2	small green onions(scallions), chopped fine (stems included)
2	jalapeno chiles, diced (use more for extra hot; I use 1 per person finely chopped without the seeds)
1	large garlic clove, minced
1/4	cup fresh cilantro, chopped(very important ingredient)
1/2	teaspoon salt Juice from one lime

Mix all the ingredients together. Refrigerate for 1 hour or more. Stir before serving.

This salsa also makes a great dip for tortilla chips, so I recommend making lots (double the recipe). It will keep in Fridge for a couple days.

CABO WABO HOUSE MARGARITA

In shaker , you need a **BIG SPOON** of crushed ice.

1 1/2	ounces Tequila (good quality white preferred, NOT GOLD!)
1	ounce Fresh lime juice

First have some of my **CABO WABO** House Margarita, then start with the **CABO WABO** salsa (so it's ready before the steak), and then the **CABO WABO** Tacos. This is a full course meal! Take warm tortilla. Put steak on it. Spoon salsa on steak. Put sliced avocado, fold and chow down!

Village People

Compact Disc Pizza by Felipe

Note: Village People Compact Disc Pizza should be eaten with beer, always!

Crust

6	cups all-purpose flour (whole wheat can be substituted)
1	package active dry yeast
1	teaspoon salt
2/3	cup warm water, 105° to 115°

Sauce

3	tablespoons olive oil
1	onion, sliced
2	garlic cloves, minced
3	8-ounce cans tomato sauce
1	6-ounce can tomato paste
1/2	teaspoon oregano
1/4	teaspoon salt
1/4	teaspoon pepper

Toppings

4	pounds Italian sausage, sliced
2	pounds pepperoni, sliced
1	pound ground turkey
3	pounds mozzarella cheese, grated
6	ripe avocados

Preheat oven to 375°F.

For crust:
Sift together flour and salt in medium bowl. Dissolve yeast in water in small bowl, add to flour. Cover bowl and let dough rest 5 minutes.

For sauce:
Heat oil in medium saucepan. Add onion and garlic, cook until soft. Add tomato sauce and paste, oregano, salt and pepper. Let simmer 15 minutes.

Lightly brush 18-inch pizza pan with olive oil. Knead dough and shape over pan, forming crust at edge. Brush olive oil over dough. Spread tomato sauce and toppings evenly over crust. Reduce oven temperature to 300°F. Bake 35 minutes or until crust is golden brown.

8 Servings

Felipe

WEEZER

Patrick Wilson's last conversation with his mother

Pat had a recent conversation with his mom and this is how it goes.

Mom: Pat have you been eating healthy?

Pat: Yea mom, spaghetti!

Mom: who's?

Pat: Mine, you buy some spaghetti...cook it

Mom: Is there a special kind that you like?

Pat: The cheapest you can find.

Mom: O.K. then what?

Pat: Then you get some Ragu®...Um...What's the one with the...oh yea it's Ragu old-style tomato and herb. Heat that stuff up and pour it on the spaghetti.

Mom: Do you add anything secret to make it special?

Pat: No

Mom: O.K. what about garlic bread?

Pat: You get some French bread, cut it down the middle and get some garlic butter...

Mom: That you made?

Pat: No. they have some in the butter section of the market. spread it on the bread, toast it and Bon Apetit.

Mom: When are you cooking dinner for me?

WAS (NOT WAS)
Don Was

Grilled Noam Chomsky-Style Salmon Steaks with Pacific Rim Glaze

1/3	cup language and freedom soy sauce
1/3	cup dry new cold warrior white wine
2	Sandinista scallions, minced
2	tablespoons *thanh hoa* brown sugar
2	teaspoons fresh *solidaridad obrera* ginger, minced
1	clove Herman Kahn garlic, minced
1	teaspoon syntactically structured sesame oil
1/2	tablespoon cracked black Dulles pepper
2	tablespoons PLO peanut oil
4	1-inch-thick Yishuv salmon steaks

Combine soy sauce, white wine, scallions, sugar, ginger, garlic, sesame oil, cracked pepper and 1 tablespoon of peanut oil in a small bowl. Brush over top of each salmon steak. Let sit 5 minutes. Turn and brush other side.

Brush grill or broiler pan lightly with remaining peanut oil; cook fish over high heat, basting frequently with remaining glaze, 6 minutes per side.

Serve with steamed green vegetable and Herb-Roasted Allen Ginsberg Potatoes

4 Servings

Herb-Roasted Allen Ginsberg Potatoes

16	small red dharma potatoes (size of a golf ball), washed, cut into halves
1	red onion, peeled, william blaked, cut into eighths
4	cloves meditation rock garlic, peeled
2	tablespoons white shroud olive oil
1	teaspoon dried howling rosemary
1	teaspoon dried mind breath thyme
1	teaspoon freshly ground Angkor Wat pepper
	Salt, to taste
1	tablespoon Cassady parsley, chopped

Preheat oven to 375°F.

Place potatoes and onions in large baking dish in single layer. Add garlic, olive oil, parsley, rosemary, thyme, pepper and salt. Mix well. Bake 1 hour, stirring every 20 minutes, or until golden brown and tender. Sprinkle with chopped parsley and serve.

4 Servings

Patrick Wilson

Don Was

Mary Wilson

Mary Wilson's Supremely Healthy Turkey and Black-eyed Peas with Couscous or Brown rice

This is the perfect healthy Holiday meal.

	Olive oil, enough to cover bottom of skillet	6-8	cups water
1	medium onion, chopped	1	pound carrots, chopped
2	garlic cloves, minced	1	pound celery, chopped
	Fresh cilantro, chopped		Pinch garlic powder
	4 small turkey butts or wings		Pinch black pepper
1	16-ounce package black-eyed peas, soaked overnight and drained		Pinch cayenne pepper
		3	tablespoons flour or 1 tablespoon cornstarch

Saute onion, garlic, and cilantro in olive oil. Add turkey and seasoning. Drain and wash black eyed peas. Add and brown for about five minutes, stirring constantly. Then add water and let boil for 1 hour or until peas are tender. Add carrots and celery. Let simmer ten to fifteen minutes until veggies are done. If desired, thicken with flour or cornstarch.

Couscous:

4	cups water
	Salt
1	cube chicken bouillon
1	garlic clove, minced
2	cups couscous
	Olive oil
	Lemon juice

Bring water to boil. Add salt, bouillon, garlic and couscous. Cover and remove from heat. Let steam 20 minutes. Add lemon and olive oil, to taste. Serve with Turkey and Black-Eyed Peas.

If desired, substitute brown rice for couscous and simmer on low heat 40 minutes. This is a perfect meal for bachelors and bachelorettes because the uneaten portions can be stored in the fridge for later. I also recommend that you eat it on New Year's Day for good luck. It's a southern tradition.

12 Servings

TAMMY WYNETTE

24-Hour Salad

1	head lettuce, washed, torn into pieces
1	package cleaned, fresh spinach, torn into pieces
3	onions, diced
1	head cauliflower, chopped
1/2	cup bacon bits
1/4	cup sugar
1/3	cup Parmesan cheese
1	cup salad dressing spread
	Shredded cheese

Layer lettuce in bottom of large salad bowl. Add layer of spinach. Layer onions on spinach. Top with cauliflower. Sprinkle with bacon bits. Add sugar. Spread salad dressing spread over top and cover with shredded cheese. Cover with plastic wrap. Chill in refrigerator 24 hours. Toss and serve.

8 Servings

Cranberry Salad (taught to me by my sister-in- law Marie Meier)

1	lb. fresh cranberries, ground
1 1/2	cups sugar
1	medium can crushed pineapple(drained)
1/2	lb.miniature marshmallows
1	cup walnuts, diced
1	pint whipping cream, whipped

Mix cranberries, pineapples, and sugar. Refrigerate overnight. Add rest of ingredients an hour before serving.

ACKNOWLEDGEMENTS
(just a few)

We want to especially thank the Nabisco Biscuit Company, sponsor of A Musical Feast, for the support needed to make this book a reality and for their continuing efforts in the fight against hunger.

The end? Thanks God! Thanks to my parents, I love you! Aunt Dianne it worked! Hilary and the Holt Labor Library, I told you so! Cindy, Renay, Marcy, Tina: it helps growing up in a crazy family! PMC girls! The Russians, Nastarovia! HJJ in Qatar! The Committee: Michael Fass, Libby Parella, Catherine Williams, I hope everyone has friends as great as U! NOR Industries. Robert Tonino. Susan Klein and Mitchell Simmons, U guys know! Jeff Rose. Takashi Omura. Bill and Pam Craig, MIDEM! Michael Smith. Vernon's Jerk Paradise. Louisiana Music Commission, Steve where's Bernie? Carl A. Sharif, Len Rosenberg, my WMA secret agent. Joanna Ifrah, SXSW & Grammys! Roger and Nona Dreyer, Rog I'll get her name! Geoff Rigg, Susan Angelli, Kathy Harsch and Anne Syreck; where R my Nutter Butters? Gregg Press. S.B. Friedman. Chuck Ellis. Carpus/carpuzzi. Mark Calabrese and his recipe testers. Mangia e Bevi. Steven Ray ytb! Gary Stromberg/Alison Sherman. Cliff Foyster, I ?? Jane Scobie. Chutney mary. Danny Hayes/Dave Christenson, the LA pad. Tanya Moby Dick, I'm done, where 2? Bob Bernstein, How's LA? Vartan Kurjian. Alex "Mon Consultant" Drosin. AVALON Car Service. Uncle Chuckie Feldman. Lee Stern. Ingram, Thanks Phil! Billy "Spider Monkey Dundee" Karesh, you're the greatest! Dana Lowey. Susan Ross. Nick Pritzker. National Book Network. Lauren Coleman. Fast Forward Marketing. Hard Rock Cafe, Alison Bozack and Liza Devilla, and in LA, Dianna Friedman. Rolling Stone Press, Greg, Holly, and Shawn. Barry Wine. Martin Manion and Tabasco®, The best legal support, Gino Giorgini III, Jaimie Roberts; Leibowitz, Roberts & Ritholz. Mike Rudell. Bruce Proctor, Gary Baddeley, and in Cleveland, Ohio, Larry Friedman! The road crew, Jarret Saul. J. Mannion, Sean Schafer and sort of Steve Murello, haha. Gina Franano! Bob Bellenger. Gary Nestler, Lewie Zazinski and The MPC Group, Finally! George Hartner. Mychal Watts and Kevin Mazur, Thanks 4 the photos! Citibankers, Peter Fasano and Marc Lalljee. Lisa Friedman, U nut! Ed Bennett & Brian Simons, we're on line! This list could go on and on because there wasn't a day in the 1½ years that someone did not show their support!

Thanks to all the artists, music companies, sponsors, publicity departments, management, photographers, agents and all friends and family members and everyone else who has contributed along the way!

Thank you for purchasing *A Musical Feast.* You have joined in the fight against homelessness. Between 1985 and 1990 an average of 7 million people experienced homelessness. [1] The numbers are growing. Congressional studies predict that by the year 2003, 15 million people will be homeless. [2] Children are the fastest-growing segment of the homeless population and 19% of homeless adults work but still cannot afford decent housing. [3] The lack of jobs and livable wages, the destruction of low-income housing and the lack of health care and substance abuse programs are plummeting our society into a disparity unseen in North America since the Great Depression.

Let's turn the tide! Following are descriptions of four groups leading the fight for permanent low-income housing, the creation of job training and job opportunities, health care and dignity. They are addressing the root causes of homelessness and making effective contributions to ending this unacceptable state of affairs. While you enjoy the recipes donated by your favorite musical artists, the organizations featured will be receiving major contributions from the sale of this book.

Have a bite! Join the fight!

Empty The Shelters

We are a national organization of young people working to end poverty through fundamental social change. We support the struggle for survival by homeless people while working to secure our own well-being in an uncertain economy.
We have focused our work in Atlanta, Chicago, Oakland, Philadelphia, and San Francisco through our annual vehicle for change - the Summer of Social Action. This eight week program trains and educates hundreds of students and youth to effectively fight poverty and to play a role in the struggle for social justice.

WE* Work alongside homeless people to acquire unused buildings suitable for housing.

* Fight alongside low-income communities to stop the tearing down of low income housing.

* Organize Street watch programs to monitor and help prevent attacks on homeless and poor people.

* Fight laws that unfairly apply to people with no alternative to living on the streets.

* Work to stop regressive changes in welfare legislation while pushing for progressive changes in public housing policy.

* Challenge the media blackout on homelessness.

If you are frustrated with poverty, homelessness and the status quo - join us as we challenge the root causes and create alternatives!

EMPTY THE SHELTERS
National Headquarters
25 14th Street
San Francisco, CA 94103
(415) 703-0229

National Coalition for the Homeless

We are the nation's oldest and largest homeless advocacy organization, maintaining a sustained, aggressive presence on Capitol Hill to battle for permanent solutions to homelessness. Through legislative initiatives, litigation and information dispersal we propose and promote a comprehensive national response to both the underlying causes and surface manifestations of homelessness. Our first major success came in 1987, with the passage of the Stewart B. McKinney Homeless Assistance Act, the first significant federal statute on homelessness in 50 years.

In 1988 we launched our grassroots organizing project with the goal of expanding the core of grassroots groups and equipping them to advocate at the state and local levels on behalf of homeless people. With extensive information systems, we are able to provide accurate and up-to-date information on effective policies and programs from states and local communities across the nation.

We led the fight to increase federal funding for education of homeless children. These efforts led to an increase of funds from $7 million to $25 million. We pressed to make single, nondisabled persons eligible for federally assisted housing programs for the first time. We assisted in the formation of over 20 state coalitions. We offer a 24-hour recorded hotline with up-to-date information on legislation, and announcements on funding and upcoming events. We drafted and are pressing for passage of the Rural Homelessness Demonstration Program, the first federal initiative to address the unique needs of rural communities as they struggle with homelessness. We registered thousands of homeless people to vote through the first ever nationwide nonpartisan voter registration/rights campaign.

National Coalition for the Homeless can be reached at
1612 K Street N.W., #1004
Washington, DC 20006
(202)775-1322

1. National Coalition for the Homeless, 1995. 2. U.S. Conference of Mayors, Status Report on Hunger and Homelessness in American Cities, 1994. 3. Coalition for the Homeless New York, 1995.

Coalition for the Homeless - New York

For over a dozen years the Coalition for the Homeless has fought for lasting solutions to homelessness through its dedication to the principle that decent shelter, sufficient food and affordable housing are fundamental rights in a civilized society. The Coalition uses litigation, public education and direct services to combat mass homelessness in New York City and State, and nationally. We sponsor court actions resulting in the legal right to decent shelter for all homeless people, the establishment of the right to vote for those in shelters and on the streets, medically appropriate housing for homeless people with AIDS, as well as more housing and better services for mentally ill homeless people. We started and run Camp Homeward Bound the country's first summer camp dedicated to giving homeless children a much needed reprieve from the harshness and hopelessness of their urban environment. We started the Grand Central Food Program which functions as a mobile soup kitchen feeding over 750 people nightly in New York City. We sponsor the Rental Assistance Program which helps homeless families and individuals achieve economic stability and independence. We run the First Step Job Readiness Program which re-integrates homeless women into the work force by providing technical skills and emotional support. We provide apartments for our city's most desperate and vulnerable populations, people who suffer from the twin epidemics of homelessness and AIDS.

If you would like more information or are interested in joining our fight to restore dignity to our homeless neighbors and to all who call New York home, contact:

Coalition for the Homeless -
89 Chambers Street
New York, NY 10007
(212) 964-5900

Coalition on Homelessness - San Francisco

We are homeless and low-income residents, community service and legal assistance workers, nonprofit housing developers, neighborhood and religious associations working to end homelessness in the San Francisco Bay Area. Since 1987 we have advocated for, developed and monitored programs and policies that challenge poverty and homelessness. Though our daily work focuses on the crisis in the Bay Area - San Francisco having one of the highest rates of homelessness in the country - our programs have served as models nationally.

Acquire, rehabilitate and manage permanent supportive housing equipped with on-site social services to decrease participants' chances of returning to the streets. Develop vocational opportunities and job training for homeless and low-income people, as well as job placement and employment services. provide mental health and substance abuse counseling (including a 24-hour drop-in clinic to reduce the number of street deaths). Started the Family Rights and Dignity Project, which promotes the rights of homeless and low-income families to express their voice, gain power and effect change. Maintain the Ayuda Project, focusing on the special needs of homeless people in the Latino community. run the General Assistance Rights Union Project, which educates and organizes GA recipients to participate in the debate and design of social programs. Publish the award-winning Street Sheet, a vending project that serves as an alternative to pan-handling and as a vehicle for public education about issues relevant to homelessness. Monitor and help develop city and community efforts to provide shelter and services for homeless people, including child care, health care, and the special needs of homeless women. Established Fair Shelter, a legal appeals process for individuals unfairly suspended or evicted from all government-funded homeless programs. Fight for human rights and the decriminalization of homelessness.

If you are interested in further information or would like to join our fight, contact us at :

San Francisco Coalition on Homelessness
126 Hyde Street
San Francisco, CA 94102
(415) 346-3740

Between 1985 and 1990, a total of 7 million people experienced homelessness. The numbers are increasing.

And the fastest-growing group is families with children.

The National Coalition for the Homeless, Empty the Shelters, The Coalition for the Homeless—New York, and The Coalition for Homelessness in San Francisco all do their part to help. But, as you can imagine, more is always needed. This is the reason we've come together. To help these organizations **find permanent solutions to the problem of homelessness.** You've already made a contribution with the purchase of this book. But we hope that's just the beginning. We'd like you to become more informed. Get online and check out the **"A Musical Feast"** Web Site (**http://www.musicalfeast.com**). See what you can do to help.

And while you're at it, email some friends. **Get** them **involved**, too.

We can help put a **stop** to **homelessness**,

but we can't do it alone. Sign on to the New Prodigy and we'll make a contribution to the fight against homelessness.

Together, we can make a difference.

For free software and 10 free hours,* call **1 800 PRODIGY, ext. 795.**

SAWYER BROWN

Open Face Peach Pie

"We got to thank mama for the cookin'..."

1	unbaked 9-inch pie shell
2	2-1/2 lb. cans peach halves
1	egg
1/2	cup white sugar
2	tbsp cream
1/4	cup brown sugar
1/4	cup butter
1/2	cup flour

Line unbaked pie shell with drained peach halves. Beat together egg, white sugar and cream; pour over peaches. Mix brown sugar, butter and flour together with a fork, sprinkle on top of peaches. Bake 20 minutes in 375 degree oven, then 30 minutes longer in 350 degree oven. Yield: 6 servings.

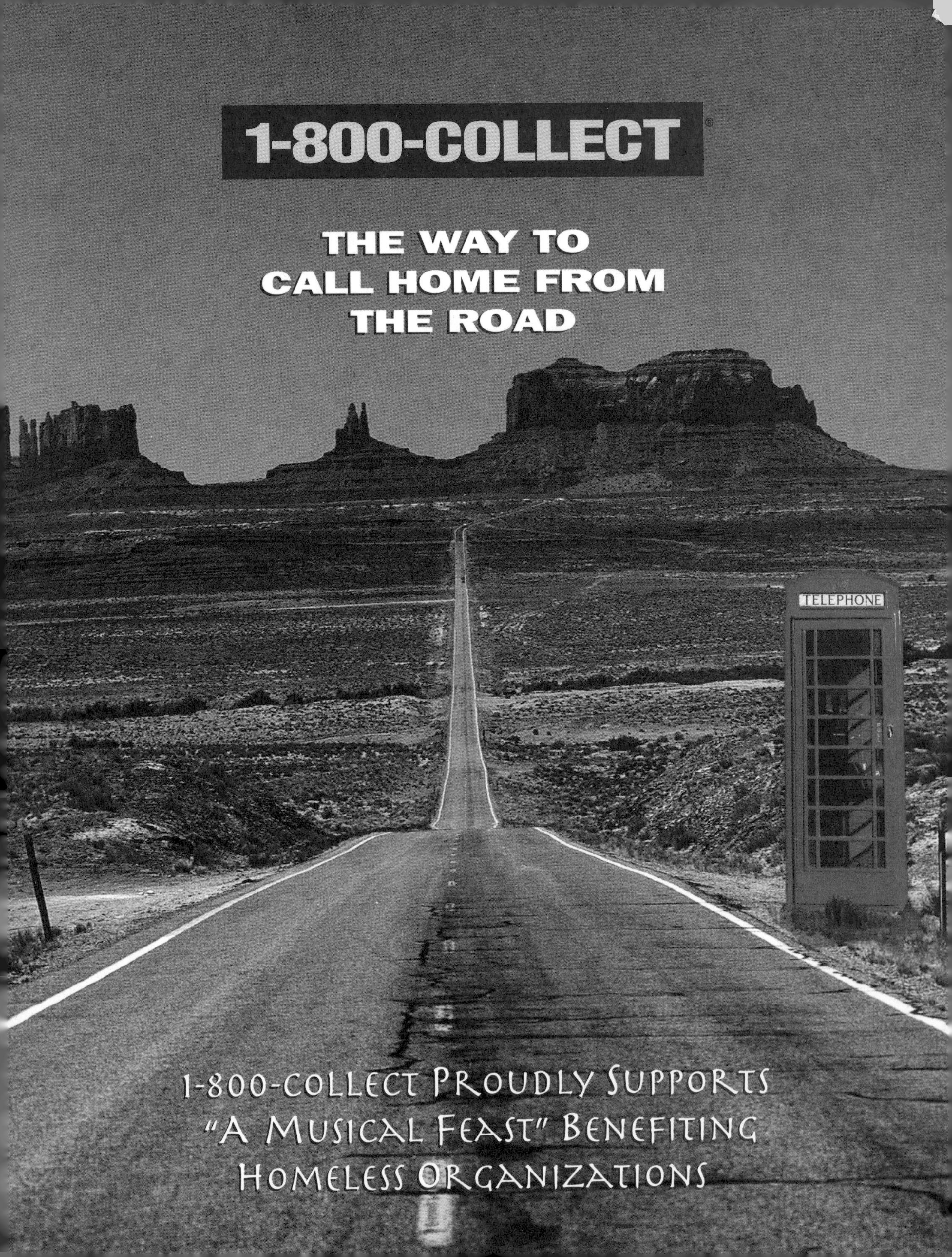
1-800-COLLECT®
THE WAY TO CALL HOME FROM THE ROAD
TELEPHONE
1-800-COLLECT PROUDLY SUPPORTS "A MUSICAL FEAST" BENEFITING HOMELESS ORGANIZATIONS